SO-ASZ-482

COLLEGE BEYOND THE STATES

European Schools That Will Change
Your Life Without Breaking the Bank

JENNIFER VIEMONT

Global Ed Press

Copyright © by 2018 Jennifer Viemont

Global Ed Press 2018

All rights reserved. No part of this publication may be
reproduced, distributed, or transmitted in any form or by
any means, including photocopying, recording, or other
electronic or mechanical methods, without the prior written
permission of the publisher, except in the case of brief
quotations embodied in critical reviews and certain other
noncommercial uses permitted by copyright law.

Although the author and publisher have made every effort
to ensure that the information in this book was correct at
press time, the author and publisher do not assume and
hereby disclaim any liability to any party for any loss,
damage, or disruption caused by errors or omissions,
whether such errors or omissions result from negligence,
accident, or any other cause.

ISBN (paperback) 978-1-7322259-0-9
ISBN (ebook) 978-1-7322259-1-6

First edition 2018

Global Ed Press
510 Meadowmont Village Circle #259
Chapel Hill, NC 27517

www.globaledpress.com

Contents

Introduction

Like many parents, I found myself worrying about college before my children had reached high school. I spoke to many parents who echoed the concerns raised in the groundbreaking documentary, *Race to Nowhere*, which explored the detrimental approaches that many well-meaning families feel pressured to use in order to prepare their children for success. Instead of success, though, this results in sleep-deprived, anxious teens who are understandably burned out by resume building and the pressure to achieve more and more—all in the name of getting into "a good college." The time to relax and discover one's own interests are scarce, or in many cases, completely absent.

When these teens finally do find themselves in college, they are faced with a new set of social issues, including binge drinking and the rape culture identified as a problem on so many campuses. There are concerns around the quality of education they are receiving as well. A recent study by the Educational Testing Service assessed literacy, numeracy, and problem-solving among millennials in different countries. They found that US students with a four-year bachelor's degree scored below their counterparts in nineteen of the twenty-one participating countries.[1] Further, the US bachelor's degree holders scored the *same* as those who had only a high school education in three of the top performing countries![2] After graduation, many are unprepared for employment or independence, so much so that the term "boomerang kids" has been coined specifically for this new phenomenon. Despite these problems, college has become a rite of passage, considered by many to be the critical stepping-stone that must be traversed if you have any hope of finding a good job.

We haven't even touched on the fact that, in recent years, college tuition has skyrocketed to levels that just a few decades ago would have seemed inconceivable. Like many parents, we had squirreled away what we could in our children's college funds. Though the national average for private university tuition is reported to be $32,000, most of the schools I looked into were closer to a jaw-dropping $50K a year! With that price tag, most middle-class families have no choice but to take on considerable debt if they want their children to obtain that four-year degree. A recent study showed that only 38% of recent college graduates felt that their education was worth the cost.[3] All these concerns were in the back of my mind when I noticed an article in my Facebook feed about an American attending college in Germany, tuition-free.

WHAT?

I was eager to find out as much as I could about college in Europe, yet my research turned up very little. This is in stark contrast to the countless number of books available about higher education here in the United States. The little information I was able to find was not clear, comprehensive, or objective. Yet I learned enough to know that this could be a viable alternative solution for those that could not afford, or simply did not want to pay, the exorbitant price of college in the United States. I knew that there were many families who would be interested in learning about these options and benefits.

I spent the next year conducting extensive research, visiting schools in Europe, talking to American students who were already attending European universities, and meeting with administrators to truly understand the experience, struggles, and benefits. I gathered information about all of the accredited English-taught bachelor's degree programs in continental Europe and in 2015, started the company Beyond the States, as a way to share this vital information with other students and families.

Prior to my research, I assumed that an international student would have to know a foreign language to study in Europe and that it would be a very expensive option. I certainly had no idea that, in non-Anglophone countries in Europe, there are more than 350 schools offering more than 1,700 full degree programs conducted entirely in English—no foreign language skills needed. Everything from the courses to the readings to the assignments are in English.

I was also wrong about cost. The average tuition international students pay for these bachelor's degree programs in Europe is around $7,000 per year. There are almost 400 programs with tuition less than $4,000 per year and fifty options that are tuition-free—even for international students.

Just like in the United States, Europe has its excellent schools, its mediocre schools, and its schools with questionable qualities. For some families, visiting schools overseas is simply not possible. Being able to evaluate a school's merit, particularly when it is outside your home country, can be difficult. Understanding the benefits to college in Europe, the differences in the systems, and potential obstacles is crucial when considering such lesser-known options.

My goal in writing this book is to make that information accessible to you, while also showing you how to save more than $100,000, opt out of the high-pressure and flawed US admissions game, and give your child a competitive advantage toward future employment. Even if you ultimately end up choosing a school in the United States, knowing these options will help you make an informed decision, as opposed to one made due to lack of alternatives.

Who Is This Book For?

This book is for anyone who is looking for an English-taught bachelor's degree program outside of their home country—either for themselves or for their children. This includes not just American high school students, but students anywhere in the world who are curious and excited to learn about other countries and cultures firsthand. Those who are seeking an alternative to the soaring cost of tuition in the United States, or who want a way to opt out of the flawed admissions process will also find this book useful. Students who are concerned about the current political climate in the United States will have the chance to learn about schools that offer the sort of education that allows one to affect real global change. And finally, this book is for *all* students—whether you're on the cusp of graduating high school or you're older, having missed out on attending or completing college the first time around. So long as you are willing to travel and step outside your comfort zone, exploring college options in Europe will show you that exciting and affordable higher education alternatives are within your grasp.

Part One: College in Europe 101

For many American parents, college in Europe is something they have never considered, for a myriad of reasons: It's too far away, their child doesn't speak the language, the cost is surely prohibitive. But as US college tuition prices continue to soar with no end in sight, many parents and students find themselves wondering if there are any viable alternatives. Consider this section a crash course in the pros, the cons, and the fundamentals of attending college in Europe.

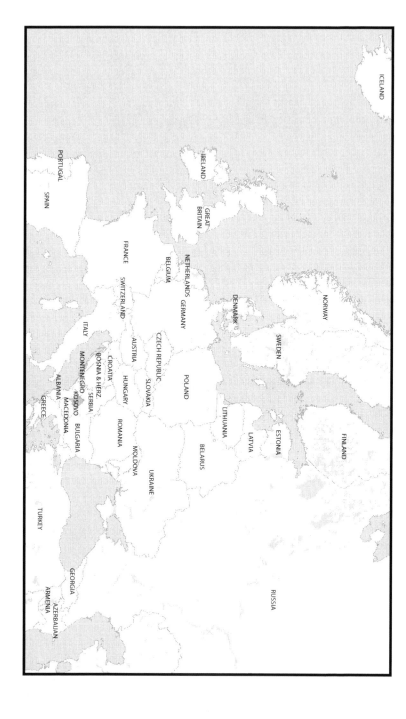

Chapter One

Benefits

"American exceptionalism had declared our country unique in the world, the one truly free and modern country, and instead of ever considering that exceptionalism was no different from any other country's nationalistic propaganda, I had internalized this belief as the basis of my reality. Wasn't that indeed what successful propaganda was supposed to do?"

— Suzy Hanson, *Notes on a Foreign Country: An American Abroad in a Post-American World*

The freedom we experience in the United States is something to appreciate. Men and women alike are free to pursue their professional, cultural, and religious interests without fear of persecution. Yet this love for our country can be taken too far, resulting in a fervent, erroneous belief of America's exceptionalism. American exceptionalism is the idea that we, as a country, are superior—our job market, our education system, our culture, our quality of life. This is a concept that has been ingrained in us, yet the truth is: American exceptionalism is a myth.

Recognizing that American exceptionalism is a myth does not mean you think poorly of your country. It does mean that you are able to acknowledge the problems and faulty systems. Doing so allows you to identify solutions, which sometimes might be found outside our country.

This fallacy of American exceptionalism is alive and well when it comes to considering college in Europe. Some will point to the US representation in global rankings as evidence of the exceptional quality of higher education in the United States. Yet they fail to look at the studies about learning outcomes or the problems with the rankings.[4,5] They believe colleges in the United States are so expensive because they offer a superior education, which will in turn lead to great employment opportunities, despite the high number of graduates who are underemployed.[6] Some believe the social experience of life on a US college campus to be indispensable, and others may simply be fearful of possible dangers that could arise when living in a new country.

It can feel hopeless to acknowledge the problems when you don't know that there are options and solutions. This chapter will explore the facts behind some of the misconceptions many people have and will look at how education in Europe can be an excellent alternative to the US higher education system.

Cost

I was vaguely aware that colleges were getting more and more expensive, though I didn't know how incredibly quickly the cost was growing until I decided to check out the trends at universities near my home. I compared current tuition with what the rates were when I went to college. In 1992, tuition at Duke University was $14,700 per year. Now, just twenty-five years later, it is $49,676. And in just five years (which will affect parents of kids currently in eighth grade and younger), it's expected to be a staggering $75,602 per year!

Even state schools have seen a drastic rate increase. In-state tuition and fees at UNC-Chapel Hill were slightly more than $1,000 in 1992 and are now almost $9,000 per year. From 1980-2010 there was an 1120% increase in tuition[7]—an increase higher than in any other good or service, including healthcare. Further, only 19% of students at American public universities graduate within four years, and even state flagship universities only have a four-year graduation rate of 36%.[8] Each extra year it takes to graduate contributes to massive amounts of student loan debt.

Compare that to the more than 300 schools in Europe (not including the UK) that offer more than 1700 English-taught bachelor's degree programs. On average, international students would pay $7,000 per year to attend one of these schools. There are almost 400 hundred programs with tuition less than $4,000 per year and fifty options that are tuition-free—even for international students. The savings are further increased when you factor in that most bachelor's programs take three to three-and-a-half years to complete. **In many cases, it costs less to obtain a full bachelor's degree in Europe, including cost of travel, than ONE year of US out-of-state or private school tuition.**

Even after accounting for housing and travel costs, the savings are immense. My son, Sam, is interested in a school in the Netherlands, Leiden University. At $12,250 a year, it is on the higher side of the tuition range in Europe. The program at Leiden takes three years to complete, which will be a total of $36,750 in tuition costs.

If Sam were to go to school in the United States, Vermont's Middlebury College would likely be a good fit for his academic interests. Yet tuition for ONE year is $52,080, which is $15,000 MORE than the full three-year program at Leiden. Let's pretend that room and board is a wash (though it's not, we will pay less than $700 for a private room and food costs as opposed to the almost $1,500 per month we would pay for a shared room and board at Middlebury) and let's not even factor in the fact that there would be travel costs for us from North Carolina to Vermont. We could theoretically fly him business class—though we won't—for the three years and still pay less for the entire cost than a year at Middlebury. Overall, our savings would be more than $171,000. Of course, if Sam were like the majority of college students in the United States, it would probably take him longer, thus making our savings even greater in Europe.

Admissions

I recently read that many college admissions counselors spend less than eight minutes on each application.[9] With so many qualified applicants, admissions counselors must often look for reasons NOT to admit an applicant. Such reasons can range from not enough AP classes, class ranking that isn't high enough, mediocre SAT/ACT scores, not enough extracurricular activities—or not enough with leadership roles—or summers that lack sufficient enrichment. It's a fine line, though, because too many extracurricular activities may indicate the applicant lacks focus, yet many extracurricular activities in a similar area might look like the applicant doesn't have a diversity of interests. The list of reasons not to admit an applicant goes on and on and is often contradictory.

The goal is to be the best, yet it's impossible to excel in every area. This sets up both students and parents to feel inadequate and vulnerable to rejection no matter what they do. US schools claim that this admissions process provides a holistic assessment of the applicants, but in fact the process is highly subjective. This competition is not just at the Ivy League schools either—many lesser-known schools, like College of the Ozarks in Missouri, Jarvis Christian College in Texas, and Rust College in Mississippi, accept less than 16% of their applicants. The stress involved with this process is linked to the increase in anxiety amongst American teenagers and is creating a national mental health crisis.[10]

Let's contrast this with the European admissions process. The first thing to recognize is that, in Europe, the schools don't use admissions rates as an indicator of educational quality or prestige. The reputation of the school is not generally linked to how selective it is. At most schools, the admissions process is less competitive, even at highly-ranked, reputable ones. Each school has its own set of admissions requirements. If you meet those requirements and there is room in the program, you are admitted. The admissions criteria might be a certain ACT/SAT score, a set GPA, a defined number of AP courses, or as little as a high school diploma. A number of very reputable European universities have programs without enrollment caps, so students who meet these criteria are accepted. Period. It doesn't matter if they have a higher GPA than the one required, or more AP courses. They aren't being compared to the other applicants; they are being assessed to see if they have the qualifications needed to succeed in the program. Students then have the first year as a student to prove that they are able to succeed. This is a process known as binding study advice (BSA), which we will take a closer look at in chapter two.

The procedures are transparent even in the schools that have more competitive admissions. There are a few schools that make admissions decisions based 100% on SAT scores. Mediocre grades? Doesn't matter. No sports? That's fine. While I don't agree that the SAT score is necessarily the best indicator of future success, I do appreciate the total transparency. This process allows students to make mistakes, to explore their interests—even those that aren't quantifiable—to spend time with family, get after-school jobs, and end the day with a good night's sleep.

Employability

Learning for learning's sake is a noble proposition, but few students go to college for reasons that don't relate to employability in some way or another. Students know that a degree is required to access many career opportunities. Why then, are our universities are not preparing students for the workforce? *There is Life After College*, by Jeffrey Selingo, notes that nearly half of college graduates in their twenties are underemployed, meaning the jobs they can get don't require a bachelor's degree. Few schools in the United States require internships or help students find them, and only 1 in 3 graduates had an internship in college, despite the fact that internships are a fast track to a job.[11] According to the Collegiate Employment Research Institute, employers hired around 50% of the interns who worked for them as full-time employees after graduation; in some fields, it is closer to 75%.[12]

Internships help students learn how to apply what they have learned in the classroom to real-world situations. Students learn relevant skills, see what others in that particular field are responsible for, and gain exposure to occupations that they might not have known about. They are able to try out an industry, role, or organization while also building contacts and gaining relevant experience for their resumes.

Bachelor's degree programs in Europe usually have at least one semester set aside for an internship. Having a semester to do internships removes many of the obstacles that students in the United States report, such as deciding between a paying summer job or a nonpaid internship, or trying to juggle internship duties and classwork. This dedicated semester also means that the internships can be completed in countries outside of the one they are studying in, increasing international opportunities and exposure.

The internship opportunities in Europe are particularly interesting and include many international companies. A number of universities have partnerships with these companies, and they will often work together to place students in appropriate internships. Some of the major internship providers are:

- Google
- BP
- JP Morgan
- Accenture

- AIG
- Deloitte
- Bayer
- Cisco
- BMW
- Skype

Many of the companies offer internships that are not just business-related, but also in engineering and science. Google, for example, offers internships related to business, software engineering, legal work, and customer service in many of their European locations.

There are also a number of organizations unique to Europe in which students can intern, such as:

- The Center for Counter-terrorism
- The International Criminal Courts in The Hague
- The World Health Organization in Geneva
- The UN Regional Center in Brussels
- European Energy in Copenhagen
- NATO Cooperative Cyber Defense Center
- The European Strategic Intelligence and Security Center

Clearly, the options are both varied and extraordinary.

Soft Skills

Along with the real-world experiences that an internship provides, prospective employers also look for an applicant's development of soft skills. Soft skills are personal attributes, as opposed to job-specific skills and knowledge. Students who have studied outside of their home country are immersed in a different culture and able to cultivate their awareness and appreciation for cultural differences. The emphasis on group work in European schools gives students the opportunity to work with people with a variety of backgrounds and perspectives. These graduates are often flexible, adaptable, and experienced in navigating unfamiliar circumstances, all of which lead to success in the workplace.[13] Employers note that soft skills are greatly lacking among US graduates and a recent study by the Institute of International Education found that studying abroad for longer periods of time has a high impact on job offers, as well as job advancement.[14]

Global Citizenship and International Exposure

"Global citizenship" is a bit of a buzzword, but it's something that is important to many individuals and families. A global citizen is one whose identity encompasses more than just their country of origin. Global citizenship means being aware of, respecting, valuing, and identifying with the world community, not just one's home country. Global citizens are just as devastated by atrocities occurring around the world as they are about those that occur in their home country, since they identify as a citizen of the world.

Interacting on a personal level with people from different countries enables a greater perspective on world events. Unlike homogeneous classrooms in the United States, the English-taught programs in Europe are developed to attract students from around the world. Classroom discussions include the perspective and experiences from these students, which allow American students to have a better understanding of the world and how current issues affect their citizens. In addition to experiencing the world by studying in a different country, students studying in Europe have many other opportunities for international experiences. The EU's Erasmus+ program, for instance, is an umbrella organization for the many programs that encourage mobility among young people. The student mobility program is one that all degree-seeking students attending European universities can participate in—even international students! Students have the opportunity to spend up to twelve months studying in other European countries (and sometimes outside of Europe as well). The attendance can be studying at another university or doing an internship in another country, or a combination of the two. There is no additional cost to these programs and students can even apply to receive a stipend of 150-500 euros per month while participating.

Many schools have their own bilateral agreements with other schools, which allow students to study in another country outside of the EU for no additional costs. Some schools have active international student organizations that plan day and weekend trips around Europe, further enhancing a student's understanding of other people and cultures.

Language Learning

Part of being a global citizen involves knowledge of another language. Multilingualism is common in Europe, as the EU has the goal for all European citizens to master two additional languages. International students are offered opportunities to learn the language of their new country. This occurs in a classroom setting and also through programs like Language Buddies and Language Cafés, where students practice conversational skills with native speakers. Some study programs involve focusing on a specific region of the world, so students also learn the language of that area. These programs usually offer an internship or study abroad in that particular region, which gives the student many opportunities to develop and apply their language learning in real-world situations.

Social Benefits

International students have peers from around the world. The cultural differences between a student from Atlanta, Georgia and one from Tbilisi, Georgia are glaring. These contrasts are recognized, openly discussed, and valued. Though there are differences in background, there are meaningful common experiences and values among international students. They are all experiencing living outside of their home country, which is a significant and life-changing experience. Further, most of these students do have the values associated with global citizenship, which connects them on a very deep level.

Any one of these benefits would provide a compelling reason to explore the options outside of the United States. When you also factor in the many problems with US higher education, it is imprudent not to consider other possibilities. It is true there are many excellent schools in the United States—I don't think anyone would argue that. There are some that have managed to look at applicants as people, and not just a

Chapter Two

Important Differences

There are different concepts and terms used around higher education in Europe. Even simple differences can be confusing if you aren't familiar with the definitions. In the United States, the term "faculty" refers to the teaching staff at a school. In Europe, the same word is used when speaking about an academic department. You may see acronyms like BSA, ESN, and ECTS and remain baffled even after finding out what they stand for. In this chapter, we will decode the terms to give you a better understanding of European higher education.

The Bologna Process and College Credits

European higher education has changed a lot in the past few decades. In 1999, education ministers from twenty-nine European countries signed the Bologna Declaration. The purpose was to create an area with comparable and understandable degrees and credits across its member states. This enabled greater mobility for students in the EU. Universities across the participating countries coordinated the duration and structure of degrees and made learning outcomes consistent, which helps with quality control. There are now forty-seven participating countries. This is also helpful to US students who get their bachelor's degrees in Europe but want to get their master's in the United States, because their qualifications and education are much more understandable to the admissions officers in the United States than in the past.

The European Credit Transfer and Accumulation System (ECTS) was also a result of the Bologna Process. This is a standardized system of cumulative and transferable credits across the EU. In the United States, credit hours are usually put in terms of classroom hours (the twelve hours of credit a student gets in a semester means that they had twelve hours of time in a classroom each week). ECTS hours are an estimate of the total amount of time the student is expected to put into the class (including classroom hours, reading, group work, studying for exams, etcetera). One full-time academic year is 60 ECTS and, depending on the school and program, it takes 180-240 ECTS to receive a bachelor's (which you might also see referred to as first cycle). Full-time students are generally in class for ten to twelve hours per week, with an additional twenty hours of study expectations outside of the classroom.

Types of Universities

In Europe, there are different types of higher education institutions. We'll take a closer look at what each of these types of schools offer.

Universities

Universities are academic and research-based. They can

award bachelor's, master's, and doctorate degrees. The educational goals are focused on research-related skills, learning to be analytical, and presenting an argument. Many of these students go straight to a master's degree program.

Universities of Applied Sciences (UAS)

The universities of applied sciences provide more of an emphasis on learning through application than through research. Internships are generally required in these programs, as the focus at UAS schools is to provide students with the skills, knowledge, and competencies needed for the professional world. Graduates can complete a master's degree program at another university of applied science or can complete the research-related courses needed to apply to a master's degree program at a research university in Europe. This is a full bachelor's degree program so graduates are able to apply to graduate schools in the United States with this degree.

University Colleges

In the Netherlands, the university colleges offer an honors-level liberal arts degree. These schools are part of a research university, but classes, living, clubs, and such are self-contained. There are additional admission requirements as well as requirements for living on campus (one to three years, depending on the school). It is important to note that this definition of university colleges applies only to the Netherlands and that the term is used differently in other countries.

Major versus Program

When you apply to a university in the United States, you are generally applying to the institution in general, and rarely need to specify your major when you apply. In Europe, you are almost always applying to a specific program, rather than the school as a whole. This basically means that you must know your major when you apply. All of your general education requirements will relate to your program, with the opportunity to explore other interest areas through your electives. There are program options for students who know broadly what they would like to study—such as business— and also for those who know that they want to study a more specific area—such as finance or international sports management. There are even options for students who want to merge more than one interest area—like business and sustainability; or business, languages, and culture; or international business and politics. There are also a number of liberal arts programs that allow students to choose their major in the second year of study.

Program Length and Structure

The majority of bachelor's degree programs at research universities take three years to complete. Programs at universities of applied sciences generally take three-and-a-half to four years. The program structure is usually well-defined, with required courses laid out for the entire program. Almost all programs have a semester (generally the first semester of the third year) set aside for the student to complete an internship, study abroad, or minor. The EU program Erasmus+ offers all students in Europe, including international students, the opportunity to study in another country with no additional fees, as well as the possibility for a monthly stipend.

Triple Crown Accreditation and Rankings

I pay very little attention to global rankings when evaluating schools in Europe. Global rankings are based almost exclusively on criteria related to research, which is different than that used for rankings like *US News Best Colleges* (which has its own lengthy list of flaws). Not only are the research-related criteria less relevant to the undergraduate experience; they disqualify certain schools from being considered in the rankings. A university of applied science, for instance, does not focus on research and thus would not be eligible for ranking consideration.

Business schools would not qualify for global rankings either, due to the research-exclusive criteria. These schools have the option of seeking international accreditations, though, in addition to those required by their country. The main international accreditations are through AACSB, EQUIS, and AMBA. While AMBA focuses only on MBA programs, AACSB and EQUIS do evaluate criteria related to the undergraduate experience. Between the two, they assess teaching methods, curriculum, internationalization, academic quality, professional relevance, interactions with the corporate world, innovation, faculty engagement, and impact. You will see the phrase *triple crown accreditation* in some of the listings in this book. To hold this honor, a school must be accredited by all three major business school international accrediting bodies, which only 1% of business schools worldwide have achieved.

Binding Study Advice (BSA)

BSA is a common practice at schools in the Netherlands and is also used at many other schools in the EU (sometimes with a different name). Instead of utilizing stringent admissions requirements, students are expected to prove that they can succeed academically during their first year. Each school has different requirements about how many classes students must pass in order to be allowed to return the second year. Many schools offer a non-binding evaluation after the first semester before the binding decision is made at the end of the year, which can serve as a warning for students who aren't on track.

Campus

Similar to some urban schools in the United States, such as New York University, the majority of campuses in Europe are decentralized, with various buildings spread throughout the town or city. However, since students have most of their classes with one academic department, this has little impact on their lives. Most academic departments at large universities are fairly self-contained and provide their students with the majority of the resources and services they need, like academic advisors, an international office, cafés—often referred to as "canteens"—and a career counseling/internship office.

Student Life

It is here that you will find the most striking differences between US colleges and their European counterparts. In Europe, the schools almost never provide housing. Student residences (dorms) are scattered throughout the city and house students from different schools. Sometimes, a school may contract with a student residence provider and hold blocks of rooms for their students, but rarely do schools own their own housing. One advantage to this system is that it creates market competition. Housing in student residences is much more affordable than in the US dorms, while also offering layouts that are more appealing.

Most of the residences provide students with their own bedroom, which sometimes has a private bathroom. There is a shared kitchen and living area for a group of students, usually no more than eight. When you consider that most US college campuses have double occupancy rooms, a bathroom shared with an entire hall, and no kitchen to speak of, the European student residences sound like a dream.

That kitchen will certainly be utilized because few European colleges offer a meal plan option. If they do, it is usually a special feature of the residence, not offered by the school. European schools have cafeterias and canteens, but are not open for every meal on every day. Shopping for groceries and preparing meals is a common part of student life and these meals often become multicultural events amongst the group of students sharing a kitchen.

Student residences host students from different schools, which contributes to the fact that student life is connected to the city more than the school. When a party is being held at a student residence, it's attended by students from different schools. The students socializing at cafés and pubs are from different schools. Some countries have versions of a Student House, which holds a student-run coffee shop and/or bar and may host concerts, events, and parties for all students of the city.

Clearly, there are many opportunities for socialization, and sometimes, the line between social outing and academics blurs. Most academic departments have study associations that provide opportunities for academic-related events as well as social events. In Denmark, the academic departments hold Friday bars where professors and students meet up on Friday afternoons and socialize over drinks.

Schools in Europe also have many student associations that can connect students with various interest groups based on religion, culture, the arts, sports, or other hobbies. International students also have an abundance of social opportunities through the Erasmus Student Network (ESN). This group works with all international students (full-degree program and semester abroad) to help acclimate them to life outside their home country.

Athletics

Sports are another area that may be tied more to the city than the school. Many schools have their own sports facilities and teams, but they are generally fairly small. More commonly, there is a Student Sports Center for the town, often with several locations and facilities. In addition to offering standard classes and activities, they also offer the opportunities for sports associations and teams, generally at an intramural level. Just because you won't be tailgating outside a big stadium for an American college football game does not mean that a sports fan will be bored in Europe. There are opportunities for spectators or participants in soccer, rugby, ice hockey, basketball, and more, with popularity generally dictated by the country.

Chapter Three
Potential Obstacles

Clearly, European colleges have numerous benefits to offer students, but it is important to know that navigating this system is not without headaches or challenges. There are still hoops to jump through, but the process tends to be more transparent and defined than how things are generally done in the United States.

Admissions Requirements

One of the first things a school wants to know is whether the high school education the applicant received is equivalent to the one they would get in the country where they are applying. The requirements vary country to country and school to school. For instance, in Italy, Norway, the Netherlands, Denmark, and some schools in Switzerland, students with a regular US high school diploma must also have at least three, and sometimes four, AP courses with scores of at least 3. In Lithuania and Germany, US students don't need the AP courses, but must submit SAT or ACT scores. Other schools across the EU may or may not require AP classes or test scores for US students, depending on the school and program and many require only a high school diploma. Good news for students graduating with an International Baccalaureate (IB) diploma—you get to bypass all these extra requirements. The specific requirements needed for an IB diploma allow students to apply to college in Europe with automatic equivalency. One less hoop to jump through!

Some schools require students to complete entrance exams. In certain instances, the SAT or ACT can substitute for these scores, but in other cases, the exams must be completed. Universities of applied sciences in Finland require students to complete entrance exams, as do certain programs at public universities in Italy. Sometimes the exams are offered in various cities around the world (which may or may not include the US) and in other cases, applicants must travel to the school to take the exam.

Proof of Means

Germany has gotten a lot of press about offering free tuition to international students (though this only applies to public universities and is no longer country-wide). There are other countries, like Norway and Iceland, that offer the same benefit and there are also a number of options across the continent that are close to free, with tuition less than $2,000 per year. Many students mistakenly think that this means the overall experience will be free. Certainly, it is more affordable, but one still has to consider travel costs, living expense, and proof of means.

Proof of means is an amount of money set by each country that students must prove that they have access to in order to support themselves for their student visa and residence permit. This amount varies from country to country. Germany requires that students show $10,850 for the year. In Norway, students need $14,435, while the total in Estonia is $5,580 for the year. Most countries fall between $6,000-10,000 per year.

The money you provide for proof of means is the money you will use to live on during the year. Some people might find it challenging to have that amount of money up front. Parents can guarantee the student by showing their own financial resources, though this often requires an abundance of paperwork. I know one family who intended to take this route and after the hassle of the paperwork, decided to instead liquidate other funds and deposit them into the secured account for their student.

Apostille/Legalization of Documents

You will likely see directions about getting your diploma legalized. Because the United States is a member of the Hague Convention, this is a fairly simple process for Americans applying to schools in most European countries. Legalization is obtained through the acquisition of an apostille stamp on your documents that can be obtained through a visit to your Secretary of State's office. This process is a bit more confusing in a few countries. The Czech Republic, for instance, requires an additional step and students must take their documents to city hall for nostrification after they arrive in the country, though some schools handle this for students.

Scholarships and FAFSA

While some schools in Europe work with the Free Application for Federal Student Aid (FAFSA), many do not. They do, however, sometimes offer other funding opportunities. At most schools in the Netherlands, incoming international students can apply for the merit-based Holland Scholarship, which is a one-time payment of 5,000 euros. In France, all students—including international students—can receive a housing subsidy, called CAF, of around 100 euros per month. Though students can't apply until they are in France, payments are retroactive to the time of the application. Finland just recently began charging international students tuition fees; however, along with the fees came a mandate that every school offer scholarship opportunities for international students. These scholarships are generally a merit-based tuition waiver for anywhere from 25-100% of tuition.

So what happens if you have money saved in a 529 account and the school you go to doesn't have a FAFSA number? This money can still be used, but you will pay taxes (at the student beneficiary's tax rate) on the withdrawal and potentially a 10% penalty. It is important to note that these fees apply only to the *gain* on the investment, not the investment itself. Other options include transferring the money to an account for a younger sibling (or other family member), or waiting to use it for graduate school.

Independence Required

Perhaps the most important trait prospective international students need to possess is a desire for independence. This is not to say that students will need to do everything on their own, but they will need to be proactive about getting the resources and information they need. Most schools offer tutoring, language learning, mental health services, career counseling, help with residence permits, and various programs to help with acclimation. If information isn't offered about these programs and services, students will have to be willing to ask around to find it.

Independence and self-discipline are also crucial when it comes to academic life. Students are expected to do a lot of studying on their own. Unlike many classes in the United States, this is ungraded work that is not monitored by the professors. The work in between classes is done to prepare for the next class discussion, as well as to prevent the need to cram for tests. The professors let students know what they need to read and do each week, but it is up to the student to actually get it done.

These days, our society often limits opportunities for independence. Many teenagers don't live in urban areas and haven't experienced navigating public transportation on their own. Parents get email notifications regularly about grades, setting up the temptation to micromanage. Teens are often too busy with academics and extracurricular activities to have an after-school job. It is understandable, then, that some American parents might have reservations about sending their child to school overseas, fearing they simply might not have the practical experience of independence needed to thrive. It's true this can be a real challenge for American teens, yet those who have not yet cultivated their independence will have many opportunities to do so in Europe. As long as they are excited by the possibilities and confident in their abilities, they too can succeed.

Chapter Four

How the Schools Were Chosen

Before we move on to the specific schools, I'd like to briefly outline the methods of selection I used. The schools in this book were carefully chosen after it was determined they met certain criteria, discussed in more detail below. I have personally visited every school featured in the following pages and would feel confident sending my own children to any of them.

The schools were chosen based on the following factors:

Cost

The schools featured in the first section cost around half of US in-state tuition price. The schools in the second section are comparable to in-state tuition, and the third section highlights schools that cost less than half of private or out-of-state tuition in the United States.

You will see prices given in USD; please note that that number is based on the conversion rate at the time of this writing. Local currency is also provided so you can calculate cost based on current exchange rates.

Educational Experience

These schools provide classroom experiences beyond lectures, access to professors outside the classroom, and/or utilize interesting or innovative educational philosophies or approaches.

Educational Outcomes

Post-graduation opportunities at these schools are high, through resources provided by the school and/or internships.

International Student Experience

The schools provide ongoing resources that assist international students and provide various social and extracurricular opportunities.

You may notice that global rankings are missing in the list of selection criteria. As noted in chapter three, the criteria used for global rankings creates an uneven playing field, disqualifying many reputable and high-quality schools. Given the emphasis of rankings in the United States, many people feel at a loss for how to evaluate schools without using that as criteria. I encourage students and families to create their own personalized ranking system based on their specific needs and priorities, which will allow them to evaluate the schools accordingly.

I've had the great fortune to be able to visit many wonderful European schools, and not all could be included in this book. Because this book is not an exhaustive list of every

European school that meets the above criteria, there are most certainly many incredible schools that are not highlighted here. Such schools could provide wonderful opportunities for some students, as a student's individual abilities and experiences may allow them to thrive at a school that does not meet the specific criteria I set out for this book. For instance, students who have already experienced living abroad may not need as many resources around the international student experience. Other students might have qualities that allow their educational needs to be met without seminars. When it comes to education, there is no one-size-fits-all prescription, yet what sets the following schools and programs apart are the resources, support, and opportunities they provide. So long as international students are motivated and resourceful, they will be able to find success and educational fulfillment at any one of the following schools.

Part Two: Practically Free!

According to the College Board, the average annual tuition for state residents at public colleges was $9,970 for the 2017-18 school year. Thus, if a student completed their degree in four years (which most do not), they would pay $39,800 total in tuition. The schools listed in this section cost around $20,000 and less for the tuition for the entire degree—almost half the cost of in-state tuition in the United States.

Chapter Five

Tallinn University of Technology

Location: Tallinn, Estonia

Number of English-taught bachelor's degrees: 5

Average annual tuition: $3,840

Duration: 3 years

Average tuition for full degree: $11,520

Estonia

I'll admit it—a few years ago I had no idea where Estonia was. I was not on top of current events as a teen—something I now deeply regret—and so I had no idea that they were under Soviet rule from 1940-1991. During this time, there were mass deportations to Siberian work camps, food ration cards, and failed attempts for independence. Since gaining independence, Estonia has undergone rapid, awe-inspiring transformations. Their advances in technology and cyber security are particularly impressive. Technological connectivity is not only valued, but internet access is an actual human right and there is free Wi-Fi across almost the entire country. They are the most connected country, with the largest 4G coverage in Europe. Of course, this Wi-Fi is needed since Estonia is an e-society, which means that almost everything—from voting to paying for parking—is done electronically.

While an e-society might be a rather abstract concept for many parents, most students will take readily to this way of life, in part because they've already experienced it in varying degrees. The hassle of losing a wallet—replacing I.D. cards, cancelling credit cards—can be taken care of easily in Estonia, because all that information is centralized and available online. Even coordinating care with various doctors would be easier, as they could quickly look up the information you don't know. It only takes three to five minutes to file taxes in Estonia, and creating a new company—which anyone can do through their e-residency offering—takes just eighteen minutes!

Estonia's technology around public safety has halved the number of deaths by accident and 93% of emergency calls are answered within ten seconds. They have other impressive technology in the works, as well. Self-driving cars are being tested and by 2020, all school-aged children will have their materials digitized and contained in an online "e-school bag". Speaking of school-aged children, all children in Estonia learn to code beginning in elementary school. It comes as little surprise that a recent study[15] indicated that their elementary education system is one of the strongest in the world.

In 2007, there was a cyber attack directed at Estonia from the Russians. Many Estonians call this a "test" of their system. Since this time, they have become the leaders in cyber security. NATO and the EU currently use the blockchain system they developed to protect against cyber threats. Estonia is also the home of NATO's Cyber Defense Center, which just launched the first data embassy that would allow them to continue to function if their systems were disrupted by crises like cyber attacks or natural disasters.

Estonia was named "the most advanced digital society in the world" by *Wired* magazine. A bourgeoning tech and start-up hotspot, it's not surprising they have been called the next Silicon Valley. Skype is one of their biggest start-up technology successes. Estonians developed the code required for Skype and sold it to eBay in 2005 for $2.6 billon. This success story inspired other Estonians to focus on technology and entrepreneurialism, resulting in such companies as Taxify and TransferWise.

Estonia borders the Gulf of Finland, Russia, and Latvia. It is a small country, about half the size of Maine, and has a population of 1.3 million, which is close to the population of Phoenix, Arizona, or Philadelphia, Pennsylvania. More than 50% of the country is covered with forest and another almost 5% by lakes. Despite the pollution created by the Soviet occupation, they were ranked first worldwide in air quality by WHO in 2011. They have been part of the EU since 2004 and have been using the euro for currency since 2011.

Tallinn

Thirty-two percent of Estonians live in the capital, Tallinn. Tallinn is an easy two-hour ferry ride from Helsinki and, given the dramatic cost in living difference, many people live in Estonia and commute to Helsinki. In addition to ferries—which can also take you to Stockholm and St. Petersburg—the Tallinn Airport is rated the third best in Europe and the ninth best in the world. Furthermore, all residents of Tallinn, including students, benefit from free public transportation.

The contrast of old and new throughout the city is striking. It is common to see a modern building constructed next to a beautiful gothic building. Tallinn Old Town is listed as a UNESCO World Heritage site. The medieval architecture and character is like stepping into a fairytale, yet right outside of the preserved city walls are plenty of modern dining and shopping options. The streets around the town square in Old Town are filled with costumed restaurant staff trying to lure tourists in to eat, but an exploration of the side streets is a really incredible experience. You will find interesting architecture, cozy cafés, cool shops selling things like handmade felt hats, and other really quirky places. A walk down a narrow, cobbled lane will lead you to the DM Bar, which is on Lonely Planet's list of top 10 weird bars. If you didn't know, the "DM" stands for Depeche Mode, the English electro synth-pop band of the 80s. It was opened by Depeche Mode fans in 1999 and has had visits (social, not performing) from the band and other celebrities.

Tallinn is old and new, colorful and brutalist, a "bite-sized" city perfect for students coming and going or staying indefinitely. Friendships are easily sustained through running into people time and time again. I will be staying indefinitely for these very reasons.
— Hunter, 20 years old, from San Diego, CA, studying international relations at Tallinn University of Technology

Living in Tallinn

Tallinn is an easy place for international students to live. Like most of the Nordic countries, English proficiency is very high, so knowledge of Estonian is not required to get around. *Business Insider* has named them one of the most affordable European cities to live in. This certainly applies to students, as rooms in the student residences start at $140 (113.70 euros) and apartments can be found in the range of $225-550 (182.73 – 446.67 euros) per month. Tallinn is known for its safety, a fact many parents will find comforting.

Of course, no place is perfect, and the obstacle international students face in Estonia pertains to the weather. The issue is not the cold or the snow but is the lack of daylight in the winter months. Some days, six hours of daylight is the most you'll get. American students might be used to waking up before sunrise, but few are accustomed to it being dark as night at mid-afternoon. Even the daylight hours are often filled with gray skies with little to no sun. Vitamin D supplements, sun lamps, saunas, winter sports, and quick weekend getaways can all help get through this time. The reward for making it through the dark winter comes with the long summer days that peak at nineteen hours of daylight in June!

Tallinn University of Technology

Tallinn University of Technology (TTU) was founded in 1918. They have 11,200 students and though they just began internationalizing in 2006, 13.5% of their student body is international, representing more than ninety nationalities. The campus is centralized and located about twenty-five minutes from Old Town. In 2014, the campus won an award from the European Rectors Club in a contest that evaluated the accommodations, sports and health facilities, use of modern technology, and student activities of different university campuses.

TTU is the first school I think of when I meet a student interested in engineering, software development, or IT. One program they offer in English is Integrated Engineering. Most engineering programs require the student to know what they want to specialize in ahead of time, and they spend the three years focusing on that specialty. The TTU program is unique in that it introduces students to industrial engineering, design and engineering, mechatronics, materials and processes for sustainable energetics, distributed energy, software engineering, and cyber security. The education students get in this program goes far beyond introductory classes. The modules on each subject provide the level of knowledge students need for entrance to master's degree programs or work in the field.

In addition to the Integrated Engineering program, TTU also offers a Cyber Security Engineering program. Students can benefit greatly from the Estonian expertise around this topic by learning skills around networking, services, programming techniques, and penetration testing techniques. By graduation, students are able to independently design, operate, and manage secure IT systems.

The most popular program with international students is the International Business program. After receiving foundational knowledge, students can specialize in marketing, finance, and accounting. The program attempts to provide students the knowledge and skills they need around both theory and practice.

The other English-taught bachelor's degree program is Law and offers students two different tracks: the law track or the international relations track. The law track includes international and European Union law, public and private law, and—of course—law and technology. It is common for international relations programs to integrate learning from various fields. Many of their programs have a strong political science focus. By combining the International Relations program with the Law program, students are provided with a strong foundation in foreign relations, international affairs, and law. Students also have the option of specializing in the Asia-Pacific region.

TTU recognizes that employers want graduates with practical knowledge, so they apply a practical approach instead of one that is primarily theoretical. Problem-based learning is utilized throughout the University, using active learning strategies with an emphasis on group work to determine solutions around case studies and problems related to their field of study. This approach leads to more meaningful learning as well as enhanced critical thinking skills. All programs consist of lectures, seminars (led by the professors), and group work. The engineering programs also include lab classes. TTU benefits from the small size of Estonia and provides their students with guest lectures from leaders in various fields.

Professors are available to help students outside of class, in meetings, and through email. Within each department, the university also has three to five consultants. They are academic advisors who help students with course planning, registration, and logistics around the program. There is also a tutoring system in place for students who need extra academic assistance. In addition, the school offers a coordinator for students with special needs and free psychological counseling.

Though social aspects of student life in Europe are generally not centered around the school, TTU offers many opportunities for socialization. International students attend orientation and are assigned to an Estonian "buddy" who helps with acclimation. Orientation consists of a number of informational sessions around topics like health insurance, academic policies, Estonian culture, public transportation, and services offered by the school. It also includes a number of social activities and parties.

In many cities, the ESN is used almost exclusively by students participating in a semester abroad. Since TTU is small, they collaborate with ESN who include international degree students in their offerings and events. ESN arranges trips to places like Lapland and St. Petersburg. They also host international dinners, parties, and pub crawls. TTU and the student union host a number of social events throughout the year as well, including formals in winter and spring, International Night, Student Eurovision, Christmas parties, end-of-semester parties, and participation in the celebration of Estonian independence.

Not all socializing involves parties, though. There are more than forty different student organizations covering interests like the arts, sports, cultures, environmental awareness, and debate, to name a few. TTU has men's volleyball, basketball, and floor ball, as well as a women's volleyball team which plays against other Estonian teams. There are also intramural opportunities in volleyball, football, floorball, tennis, basketball, badminton, and more. Additionally, there is a cycling club that gathers for evening rides and an annual three-day bike trip.

TTU not only provides resources for students during their studies, but also supports students seeking employment. The student counseling department assists both current students and alumni and provides the tools, knowledge, and resources to find a job or internship. There is an annual job fair, specifically for international students looking for jobs and internships with local and global companies. Internships are a mandatory component of all of the programs.

The school uses the exciting developments in Estonia in ways that lead to internship and employment opportunities. The Tallinn Science Park Tehnopol is home to more than 200 technology and science-based companies. These include start-ups as well as established companies that offer a wealth of opportunities for students. The school also partners with leading global companies such as Microsoft, Google, IBM, Samsung, and Mitsubishi. Cyber security specialists are in high demand both in the United States and worldwide. In 2016, the cyber security unemployment rate was 0% and there are estimates that there will be 3.5 million unfilled cyber security positions globally by 2021. Who better to learn about this from than the known leaders in the field?

In brief:

Cyber security is a rapidly growing, ever-changing field and both Estonia and TTU are at the forefront of this realm.

Students interested in pursuing a career in IT will have the opportunity here to develop and hone the knowledge and skills they need in this field where qualified workers will be in exceedingly high demand.

Admissions

Intake: Fall

Application Period: January – May 1st

Admission Decision Issued: By June 1st

Diploma Equivalence: Applicants must have a secondary education that provides eligibility for higher education in their home country. No AP scores are required for American students.

SAT/ACT: No

Entrance Exam: Online multiple-choice test for Integrated Engineering and Cyber Security programs.

English Proficiency: Non-native speakers must demonstrate English proficiency.

TOEFL: 72 (minimum 18 reading, 17 listening, 20 speaking, 17 writing)

IELTS: 5.5 (minimum 5.5 on each section)

Cambridge: 160; TTU language test

Scholarships: All programs, except for Cyber Security Engineering, offer merit-based, full tuition waiver scholarships. The waiver covers all three years of the program. After the first semester of study, students from all programs can apply for a performance scholarship, which is also merit-based. This scholarship is 100 euros ($123.31) per month. Integrated Engineering students can also apply for a specialty scholarship, which provides a stipend of 160 euros ($197.29) per month.

English-taught bachelor's degree programs:

Cyber Security Engineering	3 years	2,400 euros ($2,955.22) per year
Integrated Engineering	3 years	3,300 euros ($4,063.42) per year
International Business Administration	3 years	3,300 euros ($4,063.42) per year
International Relations	3 years	3,300 euros ($4,063.42) per year
Law	3 years	3,300 euros ($4,063.42) per year

Chapter Six

Albert Ludwig University of Freiburg

> Location: Freiburg, Germany
> Number of English-taught bachelors: 4
> Average annual tuition: $3,700
> Duration: 4 years
> Average tuition for full degree: $14,800

Germany

Germany is often the first country that comes to mind when thinking of affordable higher education in Europe, because it has many tuition-free options for international students. In most German regions, tuition at public universities is in fact free for *all* students, regardless of where they are from. Sound too good to be true? It might, until you factor in Germany's aging population, which has created a large labor shortage. Free education attracts young people who very well may decide to stay after they graduate and help fill in that gap. Germany makes this option easier than many other countries, by granting international students an eighteen-month period to stay after graduating so they can look for a job.

Germany's overall philosophy regarding education and its

accessibility focuses on the benefits of higher education as they pertain to society as a whole, as opposed to the individual. This inclusive view makes higher education a public good—extending the definition of "public" to citizens of the world. German citizens worry that instituting tuition fees for international students could eventually mean tuition fees for them, too. Citizens in Finland expressed a similar concern, but this did not prevent the Finnish government from implementing tuition fees for international students in 2017. In Germany, there are some signs that international student tuition fees will begin in the future, as universities in the Baden Wurttemberg region have already begun charging them.

Freiburg

Freiburg is a quaint, medieval city in that very region, founded in the 12th century, in the Upper Rhine area. Its proximity to the three-nation border triangle means travel to places like Basel, Switzerland, or Strasbourg, France, is a mere hour's drive away. Outdoor enthusiasts will find much to love here, a place that has been dubbed a "Green City" for its commitment to environmental sustainability and conservation efforts. Freiburg is a bike-friendly, pedestrianized city that is undeniably picturesque, with its cobbled streets and breathtaking mountain views. It also holds the distinction of being one of the sunniest and warmest parts of the country, and, perhaps unsurprisingly, uses more solar energy than any other city in Germany.

The wonderful weather and spectacular landscapes are not all Freiburg has to offer. The Black Forest is a densely wooded, forested mountain range where people can enjoy a wide range of interesting recreational options, including lakes for swimming, waterslides, wave pools, spas, thermal baths, hiking trails, amusement parks, ice-skating, and skiing. One particularly unique offering is the Barefoot Trails. These trails were created with the idea that walking over different surfaces with bare feet leads to greater awareness and mindfulness of your surroundings. Trails are made of natural materials, like hay, peat, grape stems, sawdust, wood chips, twigs, and mud. Along the way, tired walkers can enjoy footbath therapy in streams or rest in the meditation caves.

> Going to Freiburg changed my life, and I have absolutely zero doubt that deciding to study in Germany was the best decision I've ever made. Here I'm free to study what I want, to learn new languages, and to have incredible experiences with some amazing people. I would recommend Freiburg, Germany, and Europe, to any American student who wants to change their life for the better.
> — Sean Krusch, 21, from Asheville, NC

Living in Freiburg

Living costs in Freiburg are also reasonable. Single rooms in student residences range from $275 – 450 (223.33 – 365.46 euros), depending on whether the kitchen is shared with other students or private, like a studio apartment. The twenty-three cafeterias throughout the city offer full student meals from $2

– 4 (1.62 – 3.25 euros). Another interesting housing option in Freiburg is the Homestay Program. Students rent a room in a home—usually a senior citizen's home—and receive a rent reduction in exchange for completing pre-defined chores and errands. Public transportation is also affordable and even free for students every evening after 7 p.m. Students can also buy an unlimited six-month pass for ninety-four euros, which averages to less than $20 (16.24 euros) per month.

University of Freiburg

Freiburg is a student city, with students making up more than 15% of the 220,000 total population. The majority of these students are from the University of Freiburg, the seventh-oldest university in Germany, founded in 1457. Fifteen percent of the school's 25,000 students are international students, representing more than 120 countries. The University is public, but is part of the region that began tuition fees for international students in 2017. Still, tuition still remains affordable at $3,700 (3000 euros) per year.

Freiburg University started a liberal arts English-taught bachelor's degree program in 2012, which is modeled after the university colleges in the Netherlands. University College Freiburg (UCF) is a small and international department within the university, with 300 students representing forty different countries. The program offers a mix of freedom and structure, which is quite unique in Germany (as well as much of Europe). Students take core classes during the first year, which include a course on research, writing, and introductory classes to each of the majors. Core courses compose 30% of the entire program.

After the first year, students choose between four majors, all of which are interdisciplinary. Life Science majors take courses including biochemistry, cell biology, physiology, immunology, neurosciences, the behavioral and cognitive sciences, as well as biotechnology and bioengineering. The Earth and Environmental Science major focuses on human interaction with the environment with courses on ecology, sustainability, and environmental governance. The Governance major covers international relations, political science, law, sociology, and economics. The Culture and History major studies history, philosophy, anthropology, literature, and the arts. The major courses take up 40% of the total program credits.

The majority of classes students take are specifically created for and administered by the University College. Students have ample opportunity to explore other interest areas and deepen their knowledge within their major with electives, which make up 30% of the program. These courses can be taken through the University, University College, or during a semester abroad, which 80% of UCF students complete. Interestingly, Penn State is one of the schools that the University of Freiburg has a bilateral agreement with. Yet tuition at Penn States costs around $17,000 per semester as opposed to the $1,770 per semester you pay as a visiting student from Freiburg!

In Germany, many public universities feature classes made up of huge lectures, with courses graded on the final—and sometimes midterm—exam. UCF is different. While a few of the first-year classes do have lectures, they are usually no larger than ninety students. The majority of the classes are seminars with under twenty students, and some labs are even limited to eight students. The small class sizes and open atmosphere at the school lead to greater accessibility of teaching staff. More than that though, is the fact that each student is assigned a member of the teaching staff to serve as an academic advisor. Through the years in the program, students work with the advisor to plan their studies and focus on professional goals. Grades are made up of projects, assignments, papers, and tests.

Employability is difficult to assess with hard numbers for this program. Because the program started in 2012, the first class of students graduated in 2016. Further, 75% of their graduates go directly to master's degree programs. That said, there are many structures in place at UCF that do lead to overall employability after graduation, including German language learning, which can increase post-graduation job opportunities. Though all classes are taught in English at UCF, international students are required to learn German and must pass at the A2 proficiency level after the second year. Students who need help in this area can participate in language tandems in which two students with different native backgrounds help each other with language learning.

As with many schools in Europe, internships are strongly encouraged, and are considered an important part of a student's education. Students can work with their academic advisor for career planning, or utilize the resources of the University's career department, which offers internship advising, an internship database, career counseling, and access to job fairs. Students can also utilize the career services of the Welcome Center Freiburg, an organization that assists and informs non-Germans (including international students) entering the German job market.

The University of Freiburg is one of five universities that partner together in EUCOR—The European Campus. Students of any of these schools have the unique opportunity to take courses at the University of Freiburg, Karlsruhe Institute of Technology (Germany), The University of Basel (Switzerland), University of Haute-Alsace (France), and University of Strasbourg (France). Not only does this increase a student's internationalization and provide greater opportunities for networking, students enjoy the same rights and services on any of the campuses, including access to job fairs and careers services.

The University has a large international office and the University College has its own international coordinator. Between the two offices, students can get assistance with their visas, arrivals, disability services, mental health needs, and more. The International Office hosts a comprehensive three-day orientation specifically for international students, orienting them to services and structures of both the University and the city, culminating in a dinner and party.

While UCF has its own student council that organizes interest groups, parties, trips, lectures, and publishes a student magazine, the majority of students' non-academic needs are met through Studierendenwerk Freiburg (SWFR). Studierendenwerk are state-run student services offices under the German National Association for Student Affairs. Various regions have their own local Studierendenwerk office, which serves all the universities within that region. They mediate housing arrangements, run the student cafeterias and sports programs, and provide social, medical, economic, and cultural support for students enrolled in German universities. Studierendenwerk also offers services specific to the needs of international students. They facilitate a buddy program that includes pickup from the train station, help with logistics like registration and obtaining a residence permit, and orienting the student to the campus and the city and the services available in both. They also offer the Families for International Friendship program, which matches an international student with a local family who introduces the student to everyday life events and activities. This may include visits to a Christmas market, invitations to Sunday lunch, or a walk in the Black Forest. In addition, Studierendenwerk runs the International Club, which offers regular events such as parties, international cooking competitions, international film nights, cross-cultural classes and more.

In brief:

University of Freiburg provides its students with the benefits of both a broad and in-depth interdisciplinary education. Their partnership in EUCOR means students have access to four other high-quality universities, which can further enhance learning and networking opportunities.

Admissions:

Intake: Fall

Application Period: June 1st – July 15th

Admission Decision Issued: August

Diploma Equivalence: There are an abundance of different requirements the German government has for international applicants. No AP scores are required for American students. The requirements for most countries can be found here: www.daad.de.

ACT/SAT: Students graduating from American high schools require a minimum of 29 on ACT or 1360 on SAT.

Entrance Exam: No

Other: American applicants must have a minimum 3.0 GPA and four years of English, two years of foreign language, three years of social studies, two to three years or both math and science, and two academic electives.

Non-EU students are allocated 20% of the eighty spots at UCF. They generally receive four to five times more applications than spots for international students. Applicants are ranked according to their grades and then the top 150 students are evaluated through motivation letters.

English Proficiency: Non-native speakers must demonstrate English proficiency.

TOEFL: 72-94

IELTS: 5.5-6.5

Scholarships: All students, including international, can apply for the Deutschlandstipendium. This merit-based scholarship awards 300 euros per year.

English-taught bachelor's degree programs:

Liberal Arts and Science	4 years	3,000 euros ($3,697.62) per year

Majors:

- Earth and Environmental Sciences
- Life Sciences
- Governance
- Culture and History

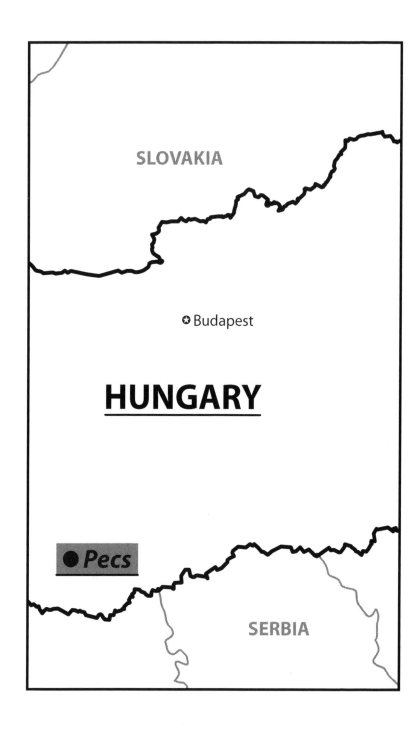

Chapter Seven

University of Pécs

Location: Pécs, Hungary

Number of English-taught bachelors: 21 (plus 4 integrated bachelor's/master's programs)

Average annual tuition: $5,865 (bachelor's degree programs only)

Duration: 3 – 4 years

Average tuition for full degree: $19,922

Hungary

Founded in 897, Hungary is one of the oldest countries in Europe and has a long and diverse history. It fell under communist rule following World War II and remained that way for forty-four years, until 1989, when Hungary finally gained its independence. It joined NATO in 1999, and in 2004 became a member of the European Union. Located in Central Europe and just smaller than the state of Indiana, Hungary is a gateway between Central and Eastern Europe, and Balkan region, bordering Austria, Slovakia, Ukraine, Romania, Serbia, Croatia, Slovenia. Though Hungary is landlocked, there are more than 10,000 hot springs, thermal baths, and medicinal spas found throughout the country.

Pécs

Pécs is the fifth-largest city in Hungary, and a three-hour train ride from the country's capital, Budapest. Because of its southwest location, Pécs has a decidedly more Mediterranean-feel as opposed to Eastern European. The Soviet influence on architecture in this part of Europe is prevalent, but Pécs, which is a 2000-year-old city, holds architectural influence primarily from the Ottoman occupation. In 1998, Pécs was given the UNESCO Peace Prize for its role with refugees during the Yugoslav Wars but the visibility of the city truly increased in 2010, when it was selected by the EU as a European Capital of Culture.

Living in Pécs

Pécs is a true student city, with students making up 15% of the 150,000 population. The University presence as well as the international student population makes it a multicultural, lively, and educated city. In fact, the number of people who speak a foreign language in Pécs is double the national average. Within the city, you can find numerous cafés and pubs, including a brewery that was founded in 1848, and produces eight kinds of beer. There are cinemas (that show English movies with Hungarian subtitles), paintball, and other popular student activities. Students can also take advantage of nearby hiking in the Mecsek Hills or trips to nearby Croatia.

The low cost of living is another reason Pécs is very popular with students.

Rooms in the student residences are doubles and quite

basic, but cost only $135 (109.53 euros) per month and include a weekly cleaning and fresh linens. There is also the option of renting an apartment with other students, which costs around $150 – $400 (121.70 – 324.53 euros) a month. Meals in the student canteen cost $2.50 – 4.00 (2.03 – 3.25 euros), movie tickets are less than $5 (4.06 euros), and a monthly bus pass is just $13.50 (10.95 euros)! Students qualify for discounts on long distance rail, paying slightly more than $10 (8.11 euros) to travel to Budapest.

The University of Pécs

Founded in 1367, the University of Pécs (PTE) is the oldest university in Hungary. The large number of programs offer an impressive variety at an incredible tuition (most are less than 5,000 euros per year). The University has been at the forefront of internationalization, offering English-taught programs for more than thirty years. This was some twenty years before the Bologna Process led to an increase in these sorts of programs across Europe, thus, PTE has become one of the most internationalized universities in Hungary.

PTE is a large university, with 20,000 students, 4,000 of which are international students, representing 105 nationalities. The school's buildings are spread throughout city, but students who stay in the dorms are generally placed in housing closest to their department. The University facilities are impressive and diverse. Some of the buildings are historic and have been renovated, while others are modern, built for the University. They are well-maintained and feature up-to-date classrooms and labs.

There are easy public transportation options for students who choose to rent an apartment in town, including a comprehensive local bus system. Cycling is a great way to get around and Pécs has marked bike lanes and a bike path that connects the University Campus and the Zsolnay Cultural Quarter, a popular area featuring many cafés, galleries, and music venues.

The University is known for the wide range of different programs it offers, and this includes offerings in English-taught degree programs. Students can choose from English-taught bachelor programs in the fields of business, sciences, humanities, and engineering. Of particular interest is the number of options they have in the health sciences, with English-taught bachelor degrees in physiotherapy, nursing, dietetics, and midwifery. These programs are four years and cost 4,000 euros (about $4,900) per year. As I dug deep into the course requirements, I was struck not only by how comprehensive the programs were, but also how much variation could be found within these particular programs themselves. Physiotherapy, for instance, includes courses that integrate other disciplines in the health sciences, like health sociology, health psychology, philosophy, and history of health sciences. In addition, there are courses on kinesiology, clinical neurophysiology, biostatistics, clinical skills, microbiology, functional analysis and examination of moving, and anatomy. Clearly, any student enrolled at Pécs who is interested in the health sciences will have a comprehensive, well-rounded, and wide-ranging field of knowledge upon completion of the program. How does this stack up against similar programs in the United States? Quite well, when you consider how rare undergraduate physical therapy majors are here in the United States; such courses are more likely to find in graduate programs.

The breadth and depth of content is found in the other health science programs too. Dietetics students study nutritional psychology, nutritional science, politics, and epidemiology, in addition to food product chemistry and biochemistry, food preparation technology, and dietetics of infancy and childhood disease. The courses for the Midwifery program include Psychosomatics of Pregnancy, Health Sociology, Alternative Medicine, Developmental Neurology, and Clinical Genetics, just to name a few. Nursing students take courses related to neurology, psychiatry, surgery, community nursing, and anesthesiology.

The University has twenty-four clinics and medical facilities where students are placed for field practice. In one semester, students spend twenty days in the field where they will complete two- to three-day field practices for each of the courses. For instance, a physiotherapy student would spend two or three days in the field learning about rheumatology, and another few days dedicated to the functional analysis of movement. These experiences require students to examine patients, make a diagnosis with a short- and long-term treatment plan, and assist with treatment exercises. Though students study medical Hungarian as part of their program, they are provided with an English-speaking interpreter during their fieldwork. In addition, students spend an entire semester completing a more comprehensive internship at the end of their studies, which can be completed in Pécs or at an institute in Frankfurt that the school has a relationship with. This opportunity is covered fully by a scholarship, and is invaluable in terms of the real-life experience students gain.

Courses generally include both theoretical lectures and a practical component. Practical courses are held in small groups of ten to twenty students, and this gives them the opportunity to practice what they have learned with demonstration dolls, moulages, and tools used in the field. This hands-on-experience provides students the opportunity to apply the knowledge they learned in the theoretical lectures. The newest curriculum includes a computer assessment at the end of each lecture. Not only does this allow for a continual assessment for the grade (as opposed to the grade consisting just of the final exam), but it also provides the professor with feedback around what needs further explanation.

The University also offers what they call "one-tier master's programs" in architecture, general medicine, dentistry, and pharmacy. These are five- and six-year programs and students graduate with both a bachelor's degree and an MSc, MD, DMD, or Pharm D. I met with students in the general medicine program who spoke of the demands related to both the entrance exam and to the program itself. One of the students had parents who went to medical school at Oxford and Harvard. She reported that even with that frame of reference, they are impressed by the rigor and curriculum at the University of Pécs. Students hoping to pursue a career in the health field in the United States should take note that they will need to pass the United States Medical Licensing Examination (USMLE). This can present a challenge, as most European schools do not prepare students for the USMLE and students themselves often find it challenging to do this on their own, due to the demands of the coursework. Both of the students I met with intend to practice in Europe after graduating, so they do not have this issue. Many students will choose this route, but those who do intend to take the USMLE usually have to take some time off to prepare for the test.

Like most schools in Europe, the different academic departments are fairly self-contained with their own international student's office, student service center, student union, and more. The student service group regularly organizes various events, parties, and excursions for the international student community. In addition, there are weekly organized parties for the students of each particular department. The department-based student unions represent students' interests and organize events with a focus on career, academics, social life, culture, or sports.

Both the University and the ESN offer orientation and buddy/mentor programs to help provide practical information, an introduction to student life, and assist with acclimation. The orientation is specifically for international students and includes information at the University and departmental level. In addition to the opportunities offered at the department and program level, the University offers a number of options for student-run organization interest clubs and events like the International Evening, Oktoberfest, and Freshman Balls. The University Sports Office offers clubs in numerous sports and also arranges competitions between the different departments.

During my visit to Pécs, I met staff in the student residences and administrators from different departments. What struck me in every single one of these meetings was how valued and well-taken care of international students are at the University. There is an office to help international students in each of the departments, as well as in the dorms. The University offers many forms of assistance to international students, including a group outing to get student residence permits, an orientation program called "Providing a Soft Landing at the University and Pécs," and a magazine for international students which is published a few times a year. There is now an initiative from the government to double the number of international students. To help ensure this, the University was given a large subsidy that has led to even more renovations, expansions, and services, and plans for international students. Such an expansion will only build upon the wide range of services and opportunities already offered. The University continues to add English-conducted programs that are of interest to international students and hold student focus groups to see what they can improve on.

In brief:

For students looking to attend a school with a wide range of English-taught bachelor's, University of Pécs is worth looking into. Those interested in the health sciences will find a wide range of variety in both the offering of programs and then within each program itself. The comprehensive, in-depth courses and the opportunities for hands-on fieldwork means those graduating from this school will have a deep, well-rounded education that will serve them well in their future careers.

Going to Europe was something I always wanted to do, yet never thought it would be possible. I was thrilled that I was able to actualize this dream when I returned to school in my mid-twenties as a student at University of Pécs. The program is exactly what I was hoping for: very analytical, and they don't cater to what's "PC" in today's standards. The curriculum is based on honest, scientific facts and discussion of theories and hypotheses is open and transparent. There's no hidden agenda, there's no bias. The coursework is rigorous and can at times be grueling, but that is necessary to achieve a high level of understanding. The professors are dedicated and will teach everything that applies to your area of study—not just what they agree with. Each subject is treated as equally important. Not to mention the University is BEAUTIFUL.

Life here is just different from the United States. It's more laid back and relaxed. I had a hard time adjusting to that different mentality here, but people and society as a whole do not rush around the way we're used to in the United States. Sure, get to class on time and make sure your assignments are completed when they're supposed to be, but if I had one piece of advice to offer US students it would be: slow down.

— Jen, age 26, from Oregon, studying
psychology at University of Pécs

Admissions:

Intake: Fall

Application Period: Applications are accepted throughout the year, with deadlines between April 30th and July 15th, depending on the program.

Admission Decision Issued: Within a few weeks of complete application.

Diploma Equivalence: Applicants must have a secondary education that provides eligibility for higher education in their home country. No AP scores are required for American students.

ACT/SAT: No

Entrance Exam: Only for dentistry, medicine, and pharmacy.

Other: Some programs require a Skype interview. Except for the programs noted that require an entrance exam, enrollment is non-selective and students who meet the admissions requirements are admitted.

English Proficiency: Non-native speakers must demonstrate English proficiency.

TOEFL: 66

IELTS: 5.5

Scholarships: No

English-taught bachelor's degree programs:

English and American Studies	3 years	3,600 euros ($4,437.14) per year
Geography	3 years	5,000 euros ($6,162.70) per year
Business Administration	3.5 years	5,500 euros ($6778.97) per year
Civil Engineering	4 years	5,500 euros ($6,778.97) per year
Midwifery	4 years	4,000 euros ($4,930.16) per year
Computer Science	3 years	5,000 euros ($6,162.70) per year
Computer Science Engineering	3.5 years	6,000 euros ($7,395.24) per year
International Relations	3 years	3,200 euros ($3,944.13) per year

Mathematics	3 years	5,000 euros ($6,162.70) per year
Biology	3 years	5,000 euros ($6,162.70) per year
Physiotherapy	4 years	4,000 euros ($4,930.16) per year
Psychology	3 years	6,900 euros ($8,504.53) per year
Physical Training	3 years	5,000 euros ($6,162.70) per year
Dietetics	4 years	4,000 euros ($4,930.16) per year
Chemistry	3 years	5,000 euros ($6,162.70) per year
Earth Science	3 years	5,000 euros ($6,162.70) per year
Physics	3 years	5,000 euros ($6,162.70) per year

Nursing	4 years	4,000 euros ($4,930.16) per year
Social Work	3.5 years	3,400 euros ($4,190.64) per year
Tourism and Catering	3 years	5,500 euros ($6,778.97) per year
Electrical Engineering	3.5 years	6,600 euros ($8,134.76) per year

One-tier master's degree programs:

Architecture	5 years	6,600 euros ($8,134.76) per year
General Medicine	6 years	13,600 euros ($16,762.54) per year
Pharmacy	5 years	9,990 euros ($12,313.07) per year
Dentistry	5 years	14,085 euros ($17,360.33) per year

Chapter Eight

Kozminski University

Location: Warsaw, Poland
Number of English-taught bachelors: 3
Average annual tuition: $6,828
Duration: 3 years
Average tuition for full degree: $20,484

Poland

Poland is the ninth largest country in Europe, and shares its border with Germany, the Czech Republic, Slovakia, Ukraine, Belarus, Lithuania, and Russia. The country's northern border meets the Baltic Sea, which is as picturesque as a coastline could be, with its sandy beaches, towering cliffs, and pristine lagoons. If you'd prefer freshwater, the Masurian Lake District, located not far from the Baltic coast, features some 2000 lakes, formed by retreating glaciers from the Ice Age. Forming a natural border with Slovakia are the Tatra Mountains, home to a wide variety of flora and fauna. Part of the Carpathian Mountains, the Tatras are the highest mountain range in this chain.

Not only does Poland possess a great deal of natural

beauty, it is also home to a great number of exquisite cities with incredible architecture and castles, some dating all the way back to the 13th century. This is not the case in Warsaw, though. More than 85% of the city center was destroyed in World War II. The Soviet Union liberated Poland from German occupation in 1944 and then took over and installed a Communist government, which ruled until 1989. Since then, the country has undergone rapid transformation as it embraced democracy and tried to rebuild its failing economy. It joined NATO in 1999 and became a member of the EU in 2004. It is now the 24th largest economy in the world. Despite this, the cost of living here is still much lower than most other EU countries. Though Poland continues to change, it is still a place of charm, steeped in history and tradition.

Warsaw

One area in the city center, Old Town, was meticulously rebuilt after the war to look like it did in the 1800s. Take a walk through Old Town—now a UNESCO site—and you'd swear it was built more than 200 years ago. The truth is though, it was built in the 1950s, and the Royal Castle wasn't completed until the 1980s. In most other areas, Warsaw lacks the architectural European charm found in so many other cities. It should be noted that air pollution can be a problem, as Poland is the most polluted country in the EU. Smog is a huge issue in the winters, primarily due to the country's heavy reliance on coal. When the smog levels are high, the city smells a bit like cigarette smoke and can lead to watery eyes and headaches.

Of course, Warsaw has many positive qualities as well, including the rapid economic development throughout the city. Tremendous numbers of international companies are moving to Warsaw, primarily due to Brexit. Citibank, Goldman Sachs, Accenture, and EY have already made the move, and Chase and JP Morgan are in the process.

Living in Warsaw

Warsaw has a population of about 2 million, with more than 270,000 students. It is a very pedestrian-friendly city with a good and easy-to-understand public transportation center. Students pay only about $16 (13 euros) for a monthly transit pass. Cost of living is also quite affordable, with a room in the student residences running around $150 (121.70 euros) while an apartment can usually be found for $250 – 375 (202.83 – 304.25 euros) per month.

Kozminski University

Though Poland is no longer under Communist rule, its impacts are still noticeable. Communism prohibits privatization, so Kozminski University, like all private universities in Poland, is relatively new. The University was founded in 1993, making it even more impressive that they hold the prestigious triple crown accreditation (see chapter two).

The adage, *Don't judge a book by its cover* is particularly relevant in Warsaw. More often than not, the exterior of buildings is not a good indicator of the interior. This certainly holds true at Kozminski. The building was bought, not built, by the

University in 1993, and the outside does not look particularly impressive. The facilities inside, however, are modern and extremely well-maintained. Kozminski is unique in that all of their facilities are on one campus and include a sports hall, two sports fields, a gym, post office, ATM machines, four cafeterias, multiple computer labs, a modern library, and a simulated courtroom for law students. A tram line right across the street can get students to the city center in about twenty minutes.

About half of the programs at Kozminski are conducted in English and 70% of the students in the English-taught programs are international students from more than seventy different countries, which makes Kozminski one of the most internationalized school in Poland. Though English is widely spoken at Kozminski, students may choose to take Polish as a second language, or German or Spanish.

Kozminski has three different English-conducted bachelor's programs that are all three years in duration. There is a Finance and Accounting program and a Management program (with specialization choices of entrepreneurship, marketing, or international management made after the first year). These programs cost $6,500 (5273.66 euros) per year and include a mandatory internship. Those specializing in entrepreneurship will have access to the Venture Lab program, where mentors from various companies help students turn their business ideas into successful ventures.

The third English-taught bachelor's degree program offered by Kozminski is a unique double-degree program in Management with Baden Württemberg Cooperative State University (DHBW) in Mannheim, Germany. Students specialize in international business and spend the first three semesters at DHBW and the last three at Kozminski. The first three months of each semester is spent in the classroom, while the last part of the semester is spent in a paid internship. It is here where students will be able to apply what they have learned in the classroom in a real-world setting. The program partners with German and Polish companies who provide the internships and also participate in selecting students for this double degree. Not only do students graduate with a bachelor's degree from each school but also with more than a year's worth of work experience in both the German and Polish markets.

Classes at Kozminski are a mixture of lectures, seminars, group work, and case studies. With 8,000 students in total, class size is small, usually no more than thirty. In addition to office hours, professors are accessible and involved formally and informally and can often be found chatting in the hallways with students.

For those of us familiar with the astronomical US prices, the tuition at Kozminski is an unheard of bargain, but in Poland it's considered a lot. Thus, Kozminski recognizes they need to provide high-end value and student satisfaction. To ensure this, they focus on combining practice with theory and developing relationships with companies around the globe.

These companies provide their students with employment, internships, lectures, networking opportunities, and workshops. Some of the companies include Accenture, Deloitte, L'oreal, Goldman Sachs, and 3M. Recruitment events occur throughout the year, with some that focus on bringing in employers from one specific country at a time. In addition, the academic coordinator and career center staff work with students individually and in groups to assist with skills around

CVs, interviewing, and aligning their education with their professional goals. With all these systems in place, it is not surprising that 90% of their graduates find work within ninety days of graduation!

Kozminski provides great supports for international students. There is a buddy program through the ESN for international students. A Kozminski University student will meet them at the airport and then take them to their housing and help them get acclimated throughout the semester. The ESN and Kozminski student council also arrange various social events throughout the year, including game nights, international movie night, bar game Olympics, cooking contests, and educational events about Polish culture. They also arrange other outings, such as trips to Krakow and Auschwitz.

Those interested in sports and outdoor activities will have plenty of options to explore. In addition to the on-site facilities, Kozminski rents out a swimming pool and a sauna, as well as basketball and volleyball courts. The school offers soccer, basketball, volleyball, swimming, tennis, table tennis, aikido, sailing, judo, two-event competition, aerobics, alpine skiing, golf, and diving.

In brief:

For such a young school, Kozminski offers its students an in-depth and diverse learning experience. Business-minded students will be able to take advantage of Kozminski's relations with myriad different companies and make excellent connections along the way.

After finishing my first year I can say that the professors not only have the education to teach but most have worked in the industry and have a lot of practical knowledge to share. The staff is great and the facilities are comfortable. The school is world-renowned and has a reputation for being one of the best. I am confident that after finishing my degree here I will have many opportunities. If you are like me and you want to see a different culture with a view totally different from the American one, then I highly recommend Warsaw and Kozminski University.

— Brandon, 24 years old, from Kentucky, studying management at Kozminski University

Admissions:

Intake: Fall

Application Period: The application process begins in May and continues through August.

Admissions Decisions Issued: Decisions are generally issued within ten days of a complete application.

Diploma Equivalence: Applicants must have a secondary education that provides eligibility for higher education in their home country. No AP scores are required for American students.

SAT: No

Entrance Exam: No

Other: Applicants must wait until they graduate to apply. The Management with Professional Placement program requires an essay and Skype interview.

English Proficiency: Non-native speakers must demonstrate English proficiency.

TOEFL: 87

IELTS: 6

Scholarships: The Kozminski Foundation offers merit-based scholarships granted as a tuition waiver of 20%.

English-taught bachelor's degree programs:

Management	3 years	21,900 PLN ($6,442) per year
Double degree in Management with Professional Placement	3 years	25,800 PLN ($7,590) per year
Finance and Accounting	3 years	21,900 PLN ($6,442) per year

Chapter Nine

Anglo-American University

Location: Prague, Czech Republic

Number of English-taught bachelors: 8

Average annual tuition: $7,265

Duration: 3 years

Average tuition for full degree: $21,795

The Czech Republic

The Czech Republic has an intriguing and complex history. The "Czech Republic" has only existed since 1993; prior to that it was part of Czechoslovakia, a state that combined the current Czech Republic and Slovakia. It was also part of the Soviet Union until its dissolution in 1989. The country has been a member of the EU since 2004 and is now a popular destination famed for its castles and dramatic architecture.

As I previously mentioned, my travels in Eastern Europe make me regret not paying more attention to current events in high school, particularly those related to the Cold War. Even still, reading about it in a book pales in comparison to meeting and interacting with people who went through these things firsthand. Such an experience really gave me a deeper understanding of the impact these global events had on people. The owners of my Airbnb in Prague were a hip, young couple in their thirties who told me of some of their experiences at the time. Matej remembers waiting in long lines for simple things like toilet paper to be rationed. His dad was in a band and had to flee the country in the 80s, as he was going to be imprisoned for playing Led Zeppelin songs. They also recalled the excitement after the largely peaceful Velvet Revolution, the period of upheaval and transition that took place from November 17 to December 29, 1989.

The Czech Republic is in the middle of Europe, bordering Germany to the west, Poland to the north, and Slovakia and Austria to the south. The country has a low crime rate and is known as one of the world's most peaceful countries. It's also one of the world's safest countries, ranked 6th safest just ahead of Switzerland and well ahead of the United States, which is 103rd out of 162.

Prague

The capital city of Prague is one of the most beautiful cities in Europe, even in the dead of winter. There is incredible architecture to be seen throughout the city, not just limited to the touristy areas. Charles Bridge is one of Prague's better-known landmarks, spanning over two thousand feet across the Vltava River. Construction of the bridge began in 1357, making it one of the oldest bridges in the world. Even older than Charles Bridge is Prague Castle, a sprawling complex estimated to have been built around 880. It holds the Guinness Book of World Records distinction as the largest castle complex in the world.

One factor I look at when assessing livability of foreign cities is the accessibility of modern day conveniences. I've stayed in some cities where I have walked endlessly just to find a place to buy Band-Aids. You will not have that problem in Prague. Supermarkets, convenience stores, and drug stores were easily found in all the neighborhoods I visited. Other services, like gyms or nail salons, were also easy to get to. The city is fairly compact and walkable, but also has good public transportation.

> Living in Prague has been a dream come true. Not only do I love studying at AAU, I have become friends with the most interesting and adventurous people who I have been able travel all over Europe with. There are so many more opportunities available to me now that I have taken the first step of moving abroad. I am so happy I took the risk of going to college in Prague because it has completely changed my life for the better.
> — Liza, age 19, from CT, studying Journalism and Communications at AAU

Living in Prague

Given all that Prague has to offer in terms of culture, history, architecture, and ease of travel to other countries in Europe, the low cost of living is truly incredible. I had to keep double-checking my currency calculator as I was sure the low costs for everything must have been due to my mental math mistakes! Life as a student is even more shockingly inexpensive. Rooms in private student residences can be found for less than $300 (242.28 euros) and a room in a nice apartment can easily be had for less than $450 (363.42 euros). Meals in the student canteens cost less than $2.50 (2.02 euros), and a monthly pass for public transportation is less than $13 (10.50 euros) for students.

Anglo-American University

There are a number of schools throughout Europe that are accredited with US agencies and use that accreditation as a justification to charge American-size tuition. I tend not to give those schools much attention. Anglo-American University interested me, though. All of their programs are conducted in English, they tout an "American" style of teaching, and they have WASC accreditation (an agency that also accredits schools like Stanford University)—yet their tuition is only $7,265 (5894 euros) per year. Like other countries in Eastern Europe, private universities were only allowed after the end of the Cold War. Though AAU is a fairly young school, founded in 1990, it is the oldest private institution of higher education in the Czech Republic. The "American" in the name is also a misnomer; it is truly an international school. Twenty percent of their 990 students are Czech, 20% are American, and the other 60% represent more than fifty-five different nationalities. The faculty is also diverse, representing twenty nationalities themselves.

AAU recently moved to a location right near the river, with a great view of the Prague Castle. The campus is located in a breathtaking Baroque palace that dates back to the 17th century. Renovations have preserved the architecture, while also ensuring modern amenities and accommodations for students.

AAU offers eight bachelor's degree programs:

- Business Administration
- International Relations
- Law
- Communication and Journalism
- Politics and Society
- Jewish Studies: History and Culture
- Visual Arts Studies
- Humanities, Society, and Culture

Though many of these programs are interdisciplinary, the Humanities, Society, and Culture program is an excellent choice for students who are unsure of what they want to focus on in their studies. This program is multidisciplinary and explores modern social issues through the fields of philosophy, religion, history, cultural anthropology, gender studies, cultural studies, and arts and literature.

Students begin by taking required courses in subjects like European history, law, economics, communication, computer information systems, politics, sociology, psychology, philosophy, and literature. After those are complete, students choose courses to further expand on their knowledge in the arts, philosophy and religion, history, and cultural studies.

The small student body does not mean that students have a limited choice of classes. More than 200 courses are generally offered each semester. Options for the Humanities program include courses like Prague Art and Architecture, The Concepts of Evil, The Jewish Experience in Central Europe, History of the Cold War and Post-Cold War Transition, Popular Culture and Media Theory, and Jews and Gypsies in Modern Europe. Students also have the opportunity to take language courses in Czech, Russian, French, Spanish, and German. Though the subjects vary widely, the learning is cohesive and culminates in the required bachelor's thesis.

In addition to theoretical knowledge, AAU emphasizes real-world experience and project-based education. Not only does real-world education occur through internships, but also through guest speakers from the field who provide a perspective other than the academic/theoretical side. The NATO in the 20th Century class is taught in partnership with the NATO Allied Command Transformation and half of each class session includes a virtual lecture from NATO representatives while the Current Issues in International Relations class brings in diplomats and ministry officials to speak. The use of project-based learning equips AAU students with skills around creative problem solving, goal setting, critical thought, collaboration, time management, and leadership skills—things that are essential for success in the 21st century.

Class size for all of the bachelor's degree programs is capped at twenty-five students, with an average size of eighteen. The small class size allows for an emphasis on interactive group work and class discussions. Students and professors to get to know each other in a way that just isn't possible with a larger student body, and professors are accessible to students inside and outside of class. This is evident through the Professors in the Pub events in which professors and students meet one evening each month in the student café and bar to have a drink and discuss a specific current world event. Topics have included hybrid warfare, migration, North Korea and nuclear threat, and the global impact of Trump.

All programs require that students complete an internship, which can be done during the summer. Internships have included work with Ernst and Young, SAP, Radio Free Europe, the US Embassy in Prague, Prague TV, and Transparency International. The Career Center helps student arrange their internship and also arranges an annual Career Expo, which has included organizations like UNICEF, Amazon, DHL, ExxonMobil, and the European Values Think Tank. Additionally, the Career Center offers the Mentorship Hub, where students or recent graduates are matched with an alumni mentor. This opens up a host of opportunities, as many AAU alumni work in places like the Foreign Affairs Department, SAP, Oracle, Nike, and Nestle, and plenty go on to start their own businesses. And while some countries make it harder for countries to hire non-citizens, the Czech Republic is not one of them. International students are able to work during their studies with no limits on hours and also have direct access to the labor market in the Czech Republic after graduating. This access has no expiration date, so students who choose to return to the United States will be able to return to work years later.

Some people might wonder if AAU's small size limits its social offerings—it does not. There are a number of organizations and groups that provide students with numerous opportunities for socialization and the chance to really immerse themselves in the culture. The Student Ambassador group offers a buddy program and events designed to help students acclimate to life as an international student in Prague. The Student Council organizes frequent parties, trips, and other events. Recent offerings have included a trip to Germany, one to the mountains, the annual ball, holiday parties, movie nights, escape room outings, paintball events, karaoke, and barbeques—something for everyone. They also oversee the student clubs at AAU, which cater to a wide variety of interests, including hiking, Model UN, basketball, and Dungeons and Dragons. Those interested can get involved with the student magazine and student radio station. Clearly, AAU's small size does not impact the wonderfully diverse number of extracurricular activities it has to offer. Of course, as is the case in most of Europe, student life is not confined to the school and extends to the events at student residences and the many cultural and social offerings throughout Prague.

In brief:

AAU is an excellent school for students seeking an in-depth, project-based education in one of the most beautiful cities in Europe. The mandatory internship requirement, the extensive alumni network, and the limitless access to the Czech Republic's labor market means students from AAU should have no problem finding meaningful employment upon graduation.

Admissions:

Intake: Fall and Spring

Application Period: Applications are accepted throughout the year. International students should apply by late April and late October in order to have time for the visa procedure.

Admission Decision Issued: The school uses rolling admissions and decisions are generally issued within three weeks.

Diploma Equivalence: Applicants must have a secondary education that provides eligibility for higher education in their home country. No AP scores are required for American students.

SAT/ACT: No

Other: Applicants must have a minimum of 2.5 GPA

English Proficiency: Non-native speakers without an IB diploma must demonstrate English proficiency.
TOEFL: 71
IELTS: 6 with a minimum of 5.5 in each section

Scholarships: Merit-based scholarships can be applied for after the first year is complete. These range from 10%-100% tuition reduction and is based on GPA.

English-taught bachelor's degree programs:

Journalism and Communications	3 years	150,000 CZK ($7,284.59) per year
Humanities, Society, and Culture	3 years	150,000 CZK ($7,284.59) per year
Politics and Society	3 years	150,000 CZK ($7,284.59) per year
Jewish Studies: History and Culture	3 years	150,000 CZK ($7,284.59) per year
Visual Arts Studies	3 years	150,000 CZK ($7,284.59) per year
International Relations	3 years	150,000 CZK ($7,284.59) per year
Business Administration	3 years	150,000 CZK ($7,284.59) per year
Law	3 years	148,000 CZK ($7,284.59) per year +University of London fees

Part Three: International Experience for In-State Prices!

In this section, we'll focus on schools that are a bit pricier, though still cost less than the average total in-state four-year tuition of $39,800. Your savings could be even greater if you're considering an out-of-state school, and even greater still when you factor in the possibility of entering the workforce and generating an income after three years of schooling as opposed to four.

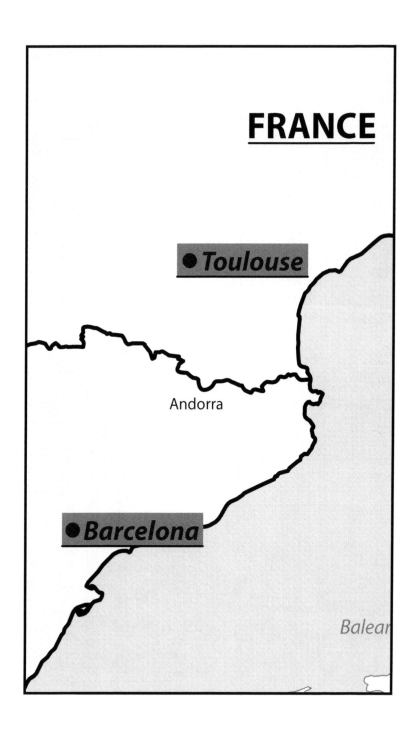

Chapter Ten

Toulouse Business School

Location: Toulouse, France; Barcelona, Spain

Number of English-taught bachelors: 1

Average annual tuition: $10,110

Duration: 3 years

Total: $30,300

France and Spain

If Germany was the first country that comes to mind for *affordable* education in Europe, then France and Spain are the two places students usually first think of when considering studying in Europe in general. Arguably the two most well-known countries in continental Europe, they also hold the distinction of being the largest countries in the European Union, home to many cities that have long since been popular with tourists. Toulouse Business School has campuses in Paris, Toulouse, Barcelona, London, and Casablanca. Currently, bachelor's students are required to study in both Toulouse and Barcelona, though Casablanca will begin offering the program in the coming years.

Living in Toulouse and Barcelona

Located in southwestern France, Toulouse is the country's fourth largest city, with a population slightly more than 465,000. It is a bustling city that has enjoyed rapid economic growth, even more so than Paris. Toulouse is commonly referred to as *La Ville Rose*, or the Pink City, thanks to all the pink-hued terra cotta that is used in much of its architecture. Those who enjoy the water can visit the River Garonne, which flows through the city, or venture farther to the Mediterranean Sea, about ninety-three miles away. Many who go to France consider a visit to Paris a must, and you can get there in about four hours by train and less than an hour by air. Forming a natural border between France and Spain, the Pyrenees is a majestic mountain range, a little more than two hours from Toulouse, which provides opportunities for numerous enjoyable outdoor activities year-round. Not quite as world-renowned as the Alps, the Pyrenees, nonetheless, has some excellent skiing in the winter and beautiful hiking trails in the summer.

With students comprising 20% of the population, Toulouse is regularly ranked as one of the top student cities in France, thanks to its rich culture, excellent weather, and overall safety for its residents. Students can also enjoy unlimited public transportation for $12.25 (10 euros). Those who would prefer to cycle in this bike-friendly city can rent a bike for the day, the week, or the month, priced at one, five, and ten euros, respectively. Students in France—including international students—are able to apply for CAF, which is student government assistance for housing. This housing assistance usually provides around $125 (100 euros) per month. The process takes approximately two or three months, but it is paid retro-actively from the time the application was submitted.

Barcelona is home to Spain's second largest student population, with more than 215,000 students. Students will find it easy to navigate the city using the excellent public transportation network. Residents of Barcelona enjoy truly phenomenal weather, with more than 300 days of sunshine per year. Most people here speak Catalan, not Spanish. Catalan is a language of its own, though some people say it sounds like a mix between Spanish, French, and Italian. In some ways, the Catalan language shares more similarities with French than it does with Spanish.

There is much natural and man-made beauty to be appreciated in Barcelona. When it comes to architecture, Barcelona is renowned for its stunning buildings and its seamless blending of the old and the new. Perhaps best known in this field was Antoni Gaudi, whose work can be described as distinctive, eclectic, and one-of-a-kind, and still today imbues Barcelona with a colorful, unique vibe.

The cost of living in the two cities is comparable, with Barcelona being slightly less expensive. Students in Toulouse can expect to pay $600 – 750 (500 – 600 euros) per month for a room in the student residence or a shared apartment. Barcelona students can find rooms in a shared apartment for less than $550 (450 euros), and rooms in the student residences start at less than $500 (400 euros) per month.

Toulouse Business School

TBS's main campus is located in Toulouse, France, with a student body of 4,500, 20% of whom are international students.

Its Barcelona campus is smaller, with around 600 students. What the Barcelona campus lacks in size, though, it certainly makes up for in diversity, as 70% of its students come from somewhere outside of France or Spain. TBS is just one of a handful of schools in Spain offering English-taught bachelor's degree programs. Many of the others are offered at public universities, where class sizes are much bigger and there are fewer resources available. This is just one of the many reasons why TBS is an excellent choice for international students seeking a bachelor's degree program in Spain.

Toulouse Business School was established in 1903 and is part of a small, elite group of schools that hold triple crown accreditation. Though the school's Management program is the only English-taught bachelor's degree program, there are many options within the program. The first choice involves where to study. Students can spend the first year in Barcelona or Toulouse. They are required to spend at least one semester of the second year at a partner university or at the Barcelona campus if they started at Toulouse, or vice versa. The location of their third year of the program is based on their chosen specializations.

The first year of the program focuses on the core curriculum, with classes in management, marketing, economics, business law, information management, and more. Students are also required to learn a language and can choose from German, Chinese, Italian, French, or Spanish. The second year focuses on international aspects of the subjects within the core curriculum, and the third year students are able to customize their program by choosing a professional path and functional competency. The third-year classes focus on the is a structured, graded part of the curriculum each year. Graduating students who are employable is important at TBS, as evidenced by the fact that 89% of their bachelor's degree students who don't go on for a master's, find work within six months of graduation. One of the main reasons for this is because TBS makes the Career Starter program mandatory. The program helps expose students to the different career options post-graduation through presentations from companies and speakers coming in to talk about their jobs. There are also mandatory classes on interviewing skills and resume writing and individual ongoing support throughout the program with an assigned mentor from the office.

But the Career Starter program plays the most important role in regard to the required internships. Each year of the program culminates in an internship, where students get to experience a different level within a company. Year one involves a two- to three-month internship with a commercial focus, where students interact with clients within a corporation. During the second year's internship, students can expect to be in an assistant management role. The internship at the end of the third year is longer at four- to six-months. This internship focuses on the specific responsibilities around the chosen competency and specialization. At the end of their studies, students have accumulated nine- to twelve-months of experience in the work place! Further, the Career Starter program makes the processes around seeking internships a true learning experience. Students have access to a database of more than 12,000 internship options, and are graded on each step, from writing a CV and cover letter, to passing a certain number of interviews, to negotiating the agreement, and presenting on the experience at the end of the internship.

In addition to the networking gained through the internships, students also benefit from access to the more than seventy companies that partner with TBS, such as Dannon, Hermes, Nestle, Louis Vuitton, Quicksilver, Deloitte, World Trade Center Barcelona, and many more. Partner companies participate in recruitment events as well as workshops and other programs offered by the Career Starter office. With all these resources, it is not surprising that so many students are finding jobs after graduating.

The Toulouse and Barcelona campuses provide extensive orientation week programs for international students, which include "welcome teams" of current students. These welcome teams will introduce international students to social life and various activities that are offered. Both campuses have an International Student Services Office to help with accommodations, visa, banking, and other logistics around living outside one's home country.

The larger Toulouse campus offers an abundance of clubs, including mountain biking, sports, cultural and artistic clubs, sustainability groups, a technology club, a group that takes regular visits to vineyards, and more. Keep in mind, though, that the majority of students in Toulouse are French; therefore, the language for many of these clubs will also be French. While the Barcelona campus has fewer clubs in number, most of their clubs and activities use English. They have a very active Student Association that organizes clubs, parties, sports, and trips.

Admissions:

Intake: Fall

Application Period: Rolling admissions. Applications accepted from October –June 30th

Admission Decision Issued: The tests and interview begin in January and students are notified with an admission offer two weeks afterward.

Diploma Equivalence: Applicants must have a secondary education that provides eligibility for higher education in their home country. No AP scores required for American students.

SAT/ACT: No

Entrance Exam: Yes. The online test assesses logical, verbal, and numerical reasoning abilities. International students can arrange to have it administered by their high school. Exam exemption is possible with a predicted IB score of 32.

Other: Skype interview is required. The acceptance rate is around 50% for international students.

English Proficiency: Non-native speakers without an IB diploma must demonstrate English proficiency.

Scholarships: Once enrolled, students can apply for a merit-based tuition reduction (25%) for their second year. In addition, the Barcelona campus awards a 25% tuition waiver to the applicant who scored highest on the admission test.

English-taught bachelor's degree programs:

Management	3 years	8,200 euros ($10,111.01) per year

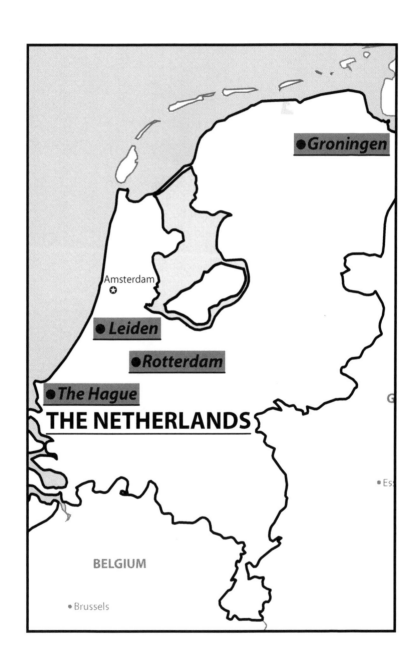

Chapter Eleven
The Netherlands

The schools highlighted in the next four chapters are all based in the Netherlands, a relatively small country that is rich in culture, history, and higher-education institutions. In this chapter, we will give you an overview of Dutch culture and their educational process, and then we'll look closely at four schools that really stand out for international students seeking an English-taught bachelor's program.

Regardless of what you plan to study in college, the Netherlands is a country that should be on the radar of all potential international students. As the first non-English speaking country in Europe to offer higher education in English, it currently holds the distinction of the greatest number of English-taught bachelor programs with over 350. While it may seem unbalanced for this book to include four schools from this country, the number of English-taught bachelor's programs here is three times as many as the other countries with the high number of English-taught programs.

The Netherlands has a reputation for being one of the most tolerant and liberal countries in Europe. It is a wealthy, highly developed nation, consistently ranked in the top ten happiest countries in the world by the World Happiness

Report. The English Proficiency Index has defined the Dutch as having the highest English proficiency of all non-Anglophone countries in the world, which makes it easy for international students to acclimate.

The country's official name is the Kingdom of the Netherlands, which is comprised of twelve provinces. Two of these provinces—Noord and Zuid-Holland—make up the area known as Holland, though the Netherlands and Holland are often used interchangeably. The Netherlands is situated in Western Europe and is bordered by Germany to the east, Belgium to the south, and the North Sea to its north and west. Its location makes it a prime spot for exploring other parts in Europe. Students can get to Paris by train in three hours and London in five hours. There are a number of airports in the Netherlands, including Amsterdam Airport Schiphol, which is one of the largest in Europe. The smaller, secondary airports such as Eindhoven, are home to several low-cost airlines.

When it comes to getting around the Netherlands, bike is most certainly the way to go. The Netherlands is a world-renowned cycling destination, and for good reason. Its flat landscape and cool climate means you can easily get around on a three-speed and not have to worry about breaking a sweat. There are four times more bikes than cars in the country, and you will find a plethora of designated bike lanes and bike parking lots.

Because more than 25% of the country is below sea level, the Dutch have an ongoing battle to keep their country from being overtaken by the sea. To do this, they have used canals and windmills as a way to control the flow of water. While the casual observer might view the windmills as one of the

Netherlands' many charming characteristics, they are actually providing an extremely important function—keeping the city from being inundated with water! This progressive and proactive approach is just one reason why Dutch firms are sought out as experts in sustainability.

The Dutch value individualism, critical thought, and frugality, while eschewing the very American/British conceit of "polite discourse." This is not to suggest they are unfriendly, but Dutch people hold being open and direct in very high esteem. These values are clearly reflected in higher education through the emphasis on group work and active participation in class. Classrooms are very interactive and students are expected to express their opinions, even if—or rather, *especially* if—those opinions differ from those of the professor and classmates. A lively debate is sure to ensue, which is part of critical thought development.

The Netherlands was one of the countries that participated in the study we noted in this book's introduction. The Dutch high school graduates outperformed our US college graduates in measures of literacy, numeracy, and problem solving. To better understand these outcomes, familiarity with the structure of the Dutch educational system is helpful.

After eighth grade, students in the Netherlands follow one of three tracks in high school: the VMBO, the HAVO, and the VWO. The VMBO is a pre-vocational education while the HAVO is the equivalent to a regular US high school diploma. The VWO is the equivalent of an IB diploma or a US high school diploma, plus four AP scores of 3+. Students without the AP scores, college credits, or an IB can apply for four-year programs at the universities of applied sciences, while students with the extra qualifications can apply to programs at the research universities or the three- or four-year programs at universities of applied sciences. There is some indication that the Dutch government may be allowing for some flexibility in how the equivalency is met. Leiden, for instance, requires only three AP courses and a GPA of 3.5. There are some programs at Erasmus University that don't require AP courses at all, though it's unclear as to how long this will be the case.

Before we dive into the differences between the schools you'll find in the Netherlands, I want to explain the admissions process as it pertains to the above qualifications. I was in the early stages of the research for my company, Beyond the States—which helps students and parents find the right college in Europe— when I visited the University of Groningen, an extremely reputable school in the northern part of the country. I met with an administrator who told me that, outside of a few programs with enrollment caps, applicants are accepted if they meet the defined criteria. I was dumbfounded. *What criteria?* I asked her. She explained that each program states what is needed—sometimes applicants might need to have certain classes (like a certain math level), English proficiency, of course, and the AP scores. The rest of our conversation went something like this:

What about GPA? When it's required, the minimum is clearly stated on the website.

What about extracurriculars? Doesn't matter.

What are SAT scores? Don't care.

What about community service? Doesn't affect the admissions decision.

What if a student has ten AP classes instead of the four?

They have the same chance of getting into a program without an enrollment cap as the student with four AP scores.

It took me quite some time to wrap my brain around this. Even the programs with enrollment caps (of which there are far less than those without) are completely transparent in their requirements. How can they do this and still provide students a rigorous academic learning environment?

A lot of this has to do with the overall philosophy about access to higher education. As is the case in much of Europe, higher education is seen to provide benefits to society as a whole. They don't want to exclude students based on indicators that have nothing to do with whether or not they can succeed academically. That said, all schools in the Netherlands utilize binding study advice. Students are required to pass a certain number of courses their first year or they are not allowed to come back to study for the second year. This allows students the opportunity to prove that they have what it takes to succeed in the program, rather than allowing their previous accomplishments (or lack thereof) to determine access to the school.

You'll find three different types of universities within the Netherlands. Universities of applied sciences (UAS) offer an education that is focused on practical knowledge. They want to ensure that their graduates are prepared for employment post-graduation by having the skills that are required for success and internships are required. After graduating, students are qualified for master's degree programs abroad—including in the United States— as well as programs at UAS schools in the Netherlands. Those interested in attending a master's degree program at a research university in the Netherlands, will first need to take certain research-related courses. These courses are required for undergraduates at research universities but not at universities of applied sciences. After completing the first year at a Dutch university of applied science, students receive a *propedeuse* certificate. This certificate can be used in lieu of AP scores and allows them to apply to most bachelor's degree programs at Dutch research universities.

Research universities focus more on preparing students for master's degree programs and require them to take courses like statistics and research methods. Remember that, until the Bologna Process, bachelor's and master's degree programs were combined. The research universities do separate the two so, while it is possible to graduate from a research university with just a bachelor's, the majority of students continue on for their master's degree. Interestingly, students who don't intend to pursue a Ph.D can get a master's degree in just one year—meaning that a student can graduate with a bachelor's and master's degree in just four years!

University colleges are the honors level, liberal arts department of a research university. These are more self-contained than most departments and have a residency requirement of one to three years, depending on the school. They also allow students to explore different fields of study and decide on their major during the second year. These programs all use selective enrollment, which means there are additional criteria along with the APs that are assessed.

What you're interested in studying is another factor that will affect what type of university you apply to. An area of study like philosophy, for instance, is pretty much purely theoretical and would only be offered at a research university.

Physiotherapy, on the other hand, requires a great deal of practical knowledge and hands-on experience, and, thus, would only be offered at a university of applied science. There are some programs that are offered at both types of schools, in fields like international business. In these cases, it is important to look at the learning style that appeals most to you as well as your future goals. In some countries, there is a certain level of academic snobbery where universities of applied sciences are seen as inferior to research universities. This is less of the case in the Netherlands where the two types of schools are viewed as different approaches as opposed to one having superiority over the other.

Clearly, the Netherlands is a country that is rich in culture and history, progressive in its approach to the environment, and a cornucopia of higher education options. Though I could fill a book on great schools in the Netherlands alone, the following four are particularly noteworthy and all stand out for different reasons.

Chapter Twelve

The Hague University of Applied Sciences

Location: The Hague, Netherlands

Number of English-taught bachelors: 11

Average annual tuition: $9,908

Duration: 3-4 years

Average tuition for full degree: $29,724 – 39,632

The Hague

Located right on the coast of the North Sea, The Hague offers the best of all worlds. With a general population of approximately 524,000 residents—30,000 of whom are students—this student-friendly city is the third largest in the Netherlands. It is conveniently located just thirty minutes from Schiphol Airport, and you can get to Amsterdam proper in slightly less than an hour.

The Hague could easily be in the running as one of Europe's most aesthetically pleasing cities. Beauty abounds as old meets new; modern and retro seamlessly blending with the historic and elegantly classic. It's a compact city and very easy to get around, especially on bike. With its diverse international population, The Hague is rightfully known as a melting pot of cultures and ethnicities, though it does have a culture that is uniquely its own. There are countless restaurants and clubs, as well as seven miles of pristine oceanfront, where you can partake in any number of aquatic sports. Those who would rather relax can do so at one of several beach bars, where you can enjoy drinks and a meal with the ocean just a short distance away. You will also find plenty of museums featuring a wide range of interests, from modern artwork to classic cars.

Globally, The Hague is known as the International City of Peace and Justice. It is home to several international courts, including the Peace Palace, which is the United Nations' International Court of Justice, and the International Criminal Court. All foreign embassies in the Netherlands are located in The Hague, as well as a number of multinational companies and many international non-governmental organizations, such as Oxfam and Save the Children.

You can also find The Hague Security Delta (HSD) here. This is a network of companies, governments, and other institutions that come together to focus on best security practices in both the digital and the real world. As one of the leaders in this field, the HSD is made up of more than 400 organizations and employs 13,400 people.

Living in The Hague

Housing in student residences generally costs between $450-600 (365 – 488.66 euros) for single rooms. Some are set up as a studio apartment with a kitchen and a bath, while others have a shared kitchen and a common area with a group of students. Many are new and more are being built to keep up with the demand. Sharing an apartment tends to be more affordable and is something many students do upon completion of their first year.

The Hague University of Applied Sciences

The Hague University of Applied Sciences (THUAS) was established in 1987 and educates 26,000 students from 140 countries. The school enrolls 5,500 students in the eleven English-taught bachelor's degree programs each year, of which almost 60% are international students.

The school offers three-year and four-year programs. The three-year programs are only for students who have VWO equivalence and include Industrial Design Engineering, International Sports Management, and User Experience Design. Students without VWO equivalence can apply for the four-year programs, which often offer a three-year option as well for those with the higher qualifications. The remaining programs are open to students without VWO equivalence. These programs are:

- International and European Law
- International Business
- International Communication Management
- International Financial Management Control
- International Public Management
- Process and Food Technology
- European Studies and Safety
- Security Management

Though THUAS has facilities in three cities, all of the English-taught bachelor's programs are offered in The Hague. The main campus building was completed in 1996 and features modern classrooms and labs, as well as a library, a restaurant, lounge areas, and a glass atrium main hall. The school recently built the Zuiderpark Sports Campus to accommodate the Sports Management Program, as well as a Dutch-taught PE program. This campus has state-of-the-art sports facilities that include beach volleyball courts, a beach soccer field, basketball court, gymnastics equipment, and more. Students can access these sports as well as those offered at the main campus for a flat rate of 99 euros per year.

Though the programs themselves cover a wide range of subjects, there are certain core aspects that are consistent throughout. Class size is small, capped at thirty, which allows greater interaction between students and with the professors. Hands-on group work and case studies that emphasize applying knowledge are utilized in all the programs. As is the case in much of the country, professors are accessible outside of the classroom for academic questions, planning, mentoring, and support. Students are assigned to an advisor with whom they are required to meet with on a regular basis. This is particularly important during that first year to ensure they are on track with the binding study advice and to put resources in place when needed.

You will find themes of peace and human rights, inter-cultural learning, world citizenship, and sustainability not just in the curriculum but also a part of administrative planning. The priorities around all these themes are represented in the acronym WIN, which guides the curriculum development and administrative decisions at THUAS.

"W" stands for *world citizen*. The education students receive at THUAS will be applicable and relevant anywhere in the world, arming them with the knowledge and skills they need to succeed globally. This is not only achieved through the curriculum, but by group work amongst an international student body and the opportunity—sometimes a requirement—to learn other languages. To facilitate this, the school offers a language buddy program in which students are paired with a native speaker who helps them practice the language they are learning.

"I" stands for *internationalization*, and is similar to that of *world citizen*. It is important that both the student body and the teaching staff are well-represented by diverse and international populations, which promotes both intercultural teaching and learning. This idea of internationalization is further enhanced for students during their semester abroad, which is always encouraged and sometimes required.

"N" stands for *networking*, which is displayed in many exciting and innovative ways, and includes internships, lectures, and case studies. THUAS collaborates with hundreds of multinational companies and organizations, and many of these relationships are reciprocal in nature. One particularly intriguing example of this reciprocity is within program development. Businesses express the need for employees in a particular area and THUAS then develops degree programs based on that. In return, these businesses provide critical feedback to the school pertaining to exactly what it is the students need to know in order to succeed upon graduating. This very symbiotic relationship is an excellent example of the way schools and businesses can work together to tailor the education experience for everyone's benefit.

All students are required to complete an internship of at least six months. This usually happens in the final months of the last year of the program and often leads directly to a job. Students benefit from the relationships THUAS has with a wide range of companies, from start-ups to NGOs to multinational organizations. Students have completed internships with Unilever, DSM, Shell, the EU, the International Criminal Court, and government agencies from around the world. Assistance with internship-related issues and future employment is provided within each program, but students can also seek help at the Career Center, which offers trainings and support as well as access to a database of employment opportunities.

But what is truly remarkable about THUAS—and the other universities of applied sciences in the Netherlands—is that graduate employment rates affect accreditation! Not only does this encourage schools to develop and offer programs that will provide students with the skills they need to succeed, it encourages them to make sure graduating students will be able to find employment in their field. THUAS conducts feasibility studies before beginning a program to ensure there is enough need to provide jobs for its students. The general rule is that 90% of bachelor's students for each program should have a job related to their program and at the appropriate level within three months of graduating.

THUAS provides a host of other resources in addition to those around academics and internships. The International Office helps students with all non-academic matters, like housing, health insurance, and immigration issues. In addition, there are offices designated to provide psychological counseling, legal counseling, and tutoring. There are many different student societies at the university, and each department has its own study association. These groups are not just for academics but also organize frequent social events. THUAS also offers a wide variety of student associations and clubs based on interest, where you can partake in things like curling, basketball, and The Hague Student Union, just to name a few.

In brief:

The core message at THUAS is: "Let's change. You. Us. The world." Forward-thinking students who want to immerse themselves in a diverse population while learning the crucial skills needed to make a real difference in the world will find a lot to appreciate at THUAS.

Since my first year at THUAS, I've learned so much just from my fellow students, as studying in such a diverse atmosphere with people from all over the world provides an education like no other. During lectures and seminars, I consume the information through the lens of my American education and upbringing, while someone sitting next to me is processing the information through the filter of their unique education and background. This leads to extremely meaningful and mind-expanding conversation; I can't count the amount of A-HA! moments I have had during seminars, just listening to discussions amongst fellow students.

It's important to know that not just the students are international, but so is the staff! Therefore, the teaching perspectives are varied and really force us students to think and consider everything we are learning.

Attending a university in Europe will, without a doubt, change you as a person. I have grown so much, in so many different ways, just by living and studying in The Hague for the past four years. If you are reading this now, you already have some interest in the world outside of the US, just like I did. Now, my thirst to see and explore and live an international life is greater than ever!

— Hannah, age 21, from New Jersey,
studying European Studies at The Hague
University of Applied Sciences

Admissions:

Intake: Fall

Application Period: October – May 1st

Admission Decision Issued: Applications are evaluated as they are received, after which an admissions decision is issued.

Diploma Equivalence: If graduating with a diploma other than an EB, IB, American High School, or British A levels, check the nuffic site (nuffic.nl) for equivalence under the overview of foreign diplomas. The three-year programs require VWO equivalence (4 AP scores of 3+ required for American high school students) and the four-year programs require HAVO equivalence.

SAT/ACT: No

Entrance Exam: No

Other: European Studies program requires that students have studied a modern foreign language.

English Proficiency: Non-native speakers without an IB diploma must demonstrate proficiency:
TOEFL: 80; IELTS: 6.0
CAE: A, B, or C (169)

Scholarships: Non-EU students can apply for the 5,000-euro Holland Scholarship for their first year of study. In addition, the students who rank highest for the Holland Scholarship will be awarded the World Citizen Talent Scholarship of 2,500 euros for the remaining years of undergraduate study at THUAS.

English-taught bachelor's programs:

European Studies	3 or 4 years	8,050 euros ($9,900.29) per year
Industrial Design Engineering	3 years	8,050 euros ($9,900.29) per year
International and European Law	4 years	8,050 euros ($9,900.29) per year
International Business	3 or 4 years	8,050 euros ($9,900.29) per year
International Communication Management	3 years	8,050 euros ($9,900.29) per year
International Financial Management and Control	3 or 4 years	8,050 euros ($9,900.29) per year
International Public Management	4 years	8,050 euros ($9,900.29) per year
International Sport Management	3 years	8,050 euros ($9,900.29) per year

Process and Food Technology	3 or 4 years	8,050 euros ($9,900.29) per year
Safety and Security Management Studies	4 years	8,050 euros ($9,900.29) per year
User Experience Design	3 years	8,050 euros ($9,900.29) per year

Chapter Thirteen

Leiden University

Location: Leiden and The Hague, Netherlands
Number of English-taught bachelors: 13
Average annual tuition: $13,126
Duration: 3 years
Average tuition for full degree: $39,378

Leiden

Taking up just nine square miles, with a population of 122,500, it could be tempting to overlook Leiden because of its small size. Yet this would be a mistake, for Leiden is an excellent example of a small-town city with the perks that a larger metropolis has to offer.

At its heart, Leiden is a student city, where students make up 20% of the population. *Vibrant* is a good word to describe the atmosphere here. Despite its small size, Leiden is visually stunning, rich in all the things one would associate with the Netherlands: tulip fields, windmills, and open-air markets, to name just a few. With almost twenty miles of canals, it should come as little surprise that Leiden has an impressive eighty-eight bridges, some of which were built hundreds of years ago.

Living in Leiden

This city certainly does not lack for amenities. You'll find three movie theaters, 154 restaurants, and seventy-four pubs. Many of these pubs are student bars, where prices are usually quite reasonable. As the birthplace of renowned 17th century painter, Rembrandt, it should come as little surprise that Leiden is known as being one of the top cities for cultural attractions and museums. The city is home to four national museums, and then a number of others, including CORPUS—Journey through the human body.

As with everywhere in the Netherlands, Leiden is easily walkable and very bike-friendly. Most students will get around by bike, and biking to the beach is a popular activity. There is also good public transportation, with three train lines and a local bus system. You can easily get to The Hague in about fifteen minutes and Amsterdam in half an hour.

International students are offered assistance with housing placement. It is not guaranteed and is provided on a first come, first served basis at a cost of around $435 (350 euros). Single rooms in the student residences generally cost between $495 – 620 (400 – 500 euros). Most of the international student accommodations in Leiden have residence advisors, common in the United States but unique through most of Europe, who can help students with support, problems, or practicalities.

The Netherlands is a great place to study because nearly everyone speaks English, but at the same time you get to experience a different culture and way of life. Since living in the Netherlands, I've fallen in love... with my bike. I love being able to ride my bike around town. Living in the Netherlands also has the added benefit of being able to travel around Europe easily, and (somewhat) affordably, as there are many budget airlines flying out of Amsterdam. I've taken advantage of my time here by traveling as much as I can (e.g., skiing in the alps of France, sunbathing in Spain, relaxing in the hot baths of Hungary).

Leiden is surely the best student city in the Netherlands (although I might be a little biased). The city is very small and quaint so it's easy to get around by bike, but it's also situated between the major cities of Amsterdam and The Hague, so it's possible to travel for day trips or go out at night. The city is extremely picturesque: the old city is surrounded by parks, and canals intertwine through and around the city. One thing I really enjoy is to kayak through these canals. Leiden is a fairly old city, so you can find historic buildings, sculptures, bridges, and windmills throughout.

I think studying abroad is an amazing experience. I have met people from every continent (except Antarctica). I learned that there is more than just one perspective; how I think is influenced by the environment that I grew up in, but other people from different places think in different ways. I also adopted some of the Dutch ideology. For example, Dutch people generally have a good work-life balance. Students strive to pass, but not necessarily to excel. I grew up thinking

the goal was to be perfect, but I've since learned that finding a balance is a much happier way to live.
— Kaitlan, age 21, from Florida, studying Psychology at Leiden University

Leiden University

Leiden University was founded in 1575 and is the oldest university in the Netherlands. Because of the city's small size, the large student population, and its decentralized campus, students often feel as if the entire city is their campus. A second campus opened in The Hague in 1990 and houses programs for approximately 4,000 students.

Leiden offers thirteen English-taught bachelor's degree programs, and expects to add three more for the coming school year. All of the programs relate to global awareness or solving problems of the world. Linguistics, South Asian Studies, Dutch Studies, Philosophy, Psychology, Archaeology, and Arts, Media, and Society programs are offered at the Leiden campus. At The Hague campus you'll find Urban Studies, International Studies, Liberal Arts, Security Studies, and International Relations and Organizations programs. They are all three years in duration with tuition of around $12,900 (10,500 euros) per year. Liberal arts majors at the University College can expect to pay slightly more at $15,600.65 (12,685 euros) per year. While the overall international student population makes up about 14% of the 29,600 students, the English-taught programs have anywhere from 30 – 80% international students, representing 115 different countries.

Leiden is one of the first schools I think of when I meet a student interested in regional studies. In addition to the South Asian and Dutch Studies programs, International Studies students choose a region to specialize in after their first year, choosing from East Asia, Africa, Russia and Eurasia, South and Southeast Asia, Latin America, North America, the Middle East, and Europe. Students in these programs look at legal, cultural, political, environmental, and historical aspects, while also learning the language of that region.

The area studies programs are the most obvious in terms of programs with an international focus, but this is something that is present throughout all of the programs. The Urban Studies program, for instance, looks at how cities around the world handle issues and challenges. They explore four different themes: the multicultural city, the safe city, the healthy city, and the sustainable city. Students take courses in each of the themes, and then choose two to specialize in. They study places like Rabat, Singapore, Montreal, and Amsterdam to see how and why they are especially multicultural, and what systems and structures are—or should be—in place to assist with the challenges cultural and linguistic diversity present. They look at Medellin, Colombia, once known as "the most dangerous place on earth" that has since reinvented itself as an innovative, eco-friendly city. Students will explore the effects of pollution in densely populated cities, like Hong Kong and New York, as they consider what urban areas can do to more efficiently and effectively use resources and improve sustainability. Clearly, this is an example not only of global awareness but also how Leiden University students are learning to solve the problems of the world.

In addition to study programs that increase global awareness, students are also encouraged to have further firsthand international experiences through study abroad. Though I believe that students should use this opportunity to explore an additional culture outside of their home country, it is fascinating to look at the cost difference of what you would pay in the United States as a study abroad student from Europe versus as a directly enrolled student. Leiden University has bilateral agreements with a number of schools in the United States, including the University of Michigan. Out-of-state students pay more than $24,000 *per semester* at Michigan but, as a study abroad student from Leiden, you will continue to pay Leiden tuition of slightly more than $6,500 (5,250 euros) for the semester.

Leiden University also shines when it comes to the support available for students. All students are assigned to a study advisor when they begin at the school. Students meet with their advisor at least two times throughout the first year to make sure they are on track for their binding study advice and to assist with getting resources in place when needed. After the first year, advisors continue to work with students to help develop post-graduation plans. Mentors who help students with academic skills are also assigned the first year. Each campus hosts open hours with the international student advisor twice a week who will help with issues such as housing, finances, or finding a doctor.

Most programs have their own study abroad and/or internship coordinator as well as a career office for the department. Students can also utilize the resources of the university-wide career office. The office offers many skill-building opportunities and access to job listings and a mentor network of alumni. This program allows students to search the mentor database and contact alumni for career advice, questions about their company, and more. In addition, there is the Young Alumni Network in which alumni under the age of thirty-five offer workshops, networking opportunities, and coaching. Though most bachelor's students will go on to enroll in a master's program, Leiden reports that 75% of their graduates find jobs in less than three months after graduating.

Both the Leiden campus and The Hague campus offer week-long orientations run by student services. Students are grouped with others from their academic department for a week of socializing, finding out about the city, and learning about services on campus. Things like setting up a bank account and buying or renting a bike can be taken care of during this week, and there are a number of fairs, pub crawls, and dinner parties meant to provide some insight into student life and the different clubs and associations available on campus.

Like most schools in Europe, each program has a study association that organizes social and academic events. Leiden students truly have an abundance of social opportunities. Besides the events organized by the study association, and the clubs and associations offered at the university level, there are also numerous activities and resources offered by the International Student Association and Leiden United, an organization whose mission is to bring Dutch and international students together. Those interested in athletics will find everything they could possibly want at the University Sports Center, which offers classes from aerial acrobatics to Zumba and everything in between. There is also a debate club,

Model UN, and groups based on interest, including cooking, music, movies, languages, theater, and photography, and more. Of course, there is no shortage of social events like parties, balls, trips, and dinners that will help foster a true sense of community and connection amongst all the students.

In brief:

Though the city of Leiden is small, Leiden University is not. The school offers a high-quality education and an abundance of student support, making it an excellent choice for anyone who wants to gain the skills and experience needed to truly make a difference in the world.

Admissions:

Intake: Fall

Application Period: October – January or April (depending on the program)

Admission Decision Issued: Generally within 4 – 6 weeks of completed application

Diploma Equivalence: American students require either an IB diploma or three AP scores of 3+ (the APs must be academic courses). If graduating with a diploma other than an EB, IB, American High School, or British A levels, check the Leiden or nuffic site (nuffic.nl) for VWO equivalence under the overview of foreign diplomas.

SAT/ACT: Include scores if taken, but it is not part of the requirement.

Entrance Exam: No

Other: American students require a minimum 3.5 GPA

English Proficiency: Non-native speakers without an IB diploma must demonstrate proficiency.
TOEFL: 90
IELTS: 6.5
CAE: A-C (180)

Scholarships: Non-EU students can apply for the 5,000-euro Holland Scholarship for their first year of study. Leiden also has a number with Sallie Mae, which opens up the option of student loans for American students.

English-taught bachelor's programs:

Archaeology	3 years	10,500 euros ($12,913.43) per year
Arts, Media, and Society	3 years	10,500 euros ($12,913.43) per year
Dutch Studies	3 years	10,500 euros ($12,913.43) per year
International Relations and Organizations	3 years	10,500 euros ($12,913.43) per year
International Studies	3 years	10,500 euros ($12,913.43) per year
Linguistics	3 years	10,500 euros ($12,913.43) per year
Philosophy: Global and Comparative Perspectives	3 years	10,500 euros ($12,913.43) per year
Political Science	3 years	10,500 euros ($12,913.43) per year

Psychology	3 years	10,500 euros ($12,913.43) per year
Security Studies	3 years	10,500 euros ($12,913.43) per year
South and Southeast Asian Studies	3 years	10,500 euros ($12,913.43) per year
Urban Studies	3 years	10,500 euros ($12,913.43) per year
*Liberal Arts and Sciences	3 years	12,685 euros ($15,600.65) per year

Majors:

- Human Diversity
- International Justice
- World Politics
- Earth, Energy, and Sustainability
- Global Public Health
- Governance, Economics, and Development

* Selective admissions procedure

Chapter Fourteen

Erasmus University Rotterdam

Location: Rotterdam, Netherlands

Number of English-taught bachelors: 11

Average annual tuition: $10,278

Duration: 3 years

Average tuition for full degree: $30,836

Rotterdam

Rotterdam is the second largest city in the Netherlands, with a population of approximately 617,000, and about 1.3 million in the entire metropolitan area. Nearly 50% of Rotterdam's population are not native to the Netherlands, or have at least one parent born outside of the country, making this truly an international city. It is also home to the Port of Rotterdam, which is the largest port in Europe, and for more than forty years was also the busiest.

Because much of the city was destroyed by Germany during World War II in what is known as the Rotterdam Blitz, architecture in Rotterdam has a decidedly more modern feel than the rest of the Netherlands. It might not evoke the post-card-perfect images of tulip fields and windmills as in other areas of the country, but it has its own unique edginess, and has been referred to as "Dutch Brooklyn" or "Dutch Berlin."

Living in Rotterdam

Erasmus University Rotterdam is unique in that it has what we think of as a true campus. The campus is a fifteen-minute bike ride from the city center, though it is also easily accessible via the tram or the metro. Here on campus you'll find a supermarket, café, a food court with a number of international offerings (even Starbucks), coffee shops, organic bakery, ATM, bike repair, book store, childcare center, and even a hair salon that offers discounts for students. The Erasmus Sports Center is also located on campus, which provides students access to a wide array of sports including tennis, rugby, soccer, basketball, and boxing, to name a few.

Campus housing consists of more than 500 rooms for full-time international students, with priority given to those in their first year. Those who are unable to get a spot on campus can find housing through the private market. Expect this to cost anywhere from around $645 – 800 (525 euros to 650 euros), though having roommates could help offset that cost.

Erasmus University Rotterdam

Erasmus University Rotterdam (EUR) was founded as an economics school in 1913. It merged with the Medical Faculty Rotterdam in 1973 and, in 2009, grew further with the addition of the School of Social Sciences. The school has triple crown accreditation and offers eleven English-taught bachelor's degree programs. EUR has a diverse student body, as 20% of the 28,000 students are international.

Though the University has a number of incredible program options, the University College is of particular interest. In the Netherlands, university colleges are the honors-level, liberal arts programs offered at a research university. The programs are kept small and they are self-contained with a required residential component to provide a true community feel within the program.

University colleges tend to provide a more broad education than the other types of schools in Europe, and they also allow students to wait to choose their major until the second year of study. That said, the number and types of majors varies greatly across the university college options in the Netherlands. Some have a limited number of theme-based options while others become less self-contained by utilizing the courses of the university to create majors. EUC has more than twenty different options for majors in the fields of economics and business, humanities, life sciences, social and behavioral sciences, and many interdepartmental and double major options. They are the only university college in the Netherlands that offer dedicated majors in economics and business.

The first year at EUC involves nine core classes and three elective choices. The academic core includes skill classes like statistics and research methods as well as interdisciplinary classes that introduce students to the various fields of study. Students are able to explore the different disciplines more specifically through three electives they take their first year. After the first year is completed, they decide on a major, which is the focus of the second year, in addition to continued research-focused studies. EUC students are able to take up to 50% of their courses outside of their major, which allows for further exploration of interest areas. During the third year, students can study abroad, complete an internship, or choose a minor. The year ends with a capstone project, which is similar to a bachelor's thesis. There is a great deal of freedom here as students pick their own unique topic within their major, working closely with an assigned professor for the duration of the project.

Problem-based learning is utilized throughout the program, which gives students the opportunity to apply the knowledge learned in lectures and readings to an actual problem. The majority of class time the first year is spent in classes no bigger than twelve, which ensures that students are actively engaged in the learning process. They learn to define problems, brainstorm hypotheses and solutions, and debate around these solutions. This process continues the second year through independent small group work. Ten percent of the final grade is based on the quantity and quality of this group participation, while the other 90% of the grade is composed of multiple assignments, tests, and projects.

Like in most Dutch classrooms, students are encouraged to provide different perspectives and opinions from those expressed by their classmates and professors. Given that 50% of students at EUC are international, these open discussions provide the opportunity for greater global awareness, often through firsthand accounts. While learning about the Israeli/Palestinian conflict from the pages of a textbook would give students some knowledge and understanding of the topic, hearing about it from someone who has lived through it pro-vides a type of learning experience a textbook is simply not capable of delivering.

EUC also encourages global citizenship through the Language and Training Center (LTC), which is part of the University's Service Center. The LTC provides students access to a wide range of foreign languages, through language courses, language tests, and communication skills courses. EUC reimburses students for the cost of the courses, clearly showing how much they value the their students development as world citizens.

Along with all EUR students, EUC students have the oppor-tunity to graduate with a double degree in philosophy. Doing so would only require one additional year and about $2,700 (2,200 euros). Students who select this option are able to study philosophy in relation to their primary area of study, which makes the learning in both areas more meaningful.

The Rotterdam Arts and Science Lab (RASL) is a double degree option accessible only to EUC students and those in the University's Arts and Culture Studies program. The school collaborates with Codarts and Rotterdam University of Applied Sciences to allow their students to graduate with degrees from both schools in just five years. This allows students to study music, fine arts, photography, advertising, animation, audio-visual design, fashion design, illustration, lifestyle, produce design, or spatial design in addition to their program at EUC.

The University College building is located about ten min-utes by bike from the main campus. The building itself is one of the most impressive school facilities I have visited. It's right in the middle of the city and is one of the few buildings that survived WWII. It was originally a library but was turned into a museum after the war. When converting it to a school, EUC did a fantastic job of preserving the history while also providing modern amenities. There are impressive details throughout the building like marble floors and pillars, rich woodwork, and stained glass, mixed with funky modern light fixtures and skylights.

EUC students have a residency requirement for the first year. Not only does this allow the benefit of getting to know the other students in the program, but it means that housing is guaranteed, eliminating the potential headache of securing housing from abroad. EUC recently opened their new housing facilities, which are right in the city center, about a ten-minute walk from the building. Though housing is on the higher end of the range, at around $740 (600 euros) per month, students have their own furnished studio apartment, with ample common space to socialize with other EUC students.

All EUC students are assigned to a student counselor, who follows them throughout their entire program. Students meet individually with their counselor at least twice a year for academic planning, or to get assistance with academic or personal issues. The main university also provides all students access to the university psychologists, who offer individual therapy in addition to group sessions around time management and stress management.

EUC has a Student Life Officer who helps facilitate the community environment, assists with housing for second-year students, and arranges an orientation program for new EUC students. EUC has its own student association with committees that plan events and organize clubs around sports, music, cultural cooking, film and photography, and theater. Of course, they also plan many parties and social events. EUC students can take advantage of all the resources, including social opportunities, provided by the parent University (EUR). The school offers everything from ladies' hip-hop night to a theater performance about the economy of warfare to dating events. The student association offerings run the gamut as well, from an international women's group, social groups, travel, political, LGBT, and cultural groups.

All Erasmus University students, including EUC students, have an abundance of orientation opportunities through the University and an ESN. The Buddy Program includes pick up at the Amsterdam airport and follows with activities including lectures, parties, free introductory Dutch classes, campus tours, and information about sports and social opportunities. Students are put in groups of fifteen with others from their program, led by a guide from that program as well. The University also offers international students a "One Stop Shop" which allows students to handle logistics like registering with the appropriate Dutch government organizations, getting insurance, renting a bike, and opening a bank account all in one place. The ESN orientation is more social in nature, including meals, parties, beer tasting, and bike lessons.

In brief:

With EUC's small classes and emphasis on problem-based learning, students are expected to not just be active participants but leaders in their own education. Erasmus University

Rotterdam is a world-class research institute, providing its students with a high-quality education and the tools and resources needed to become global citizens.

My experience at EUC has been amazing. EUC has such an open, inclusive atmosphere, thanks to the faculty and the students. The faculty is always very approachable and willing to help. Another thing I really liked was that the tutors and the lecturers are often people who are still working in their field and clearly have a passion for the subject. The community of students is close-knit and diverse. It's so easy to find your niche, and I've met some of my best friends here.

I find the project-based learning style extremely helpful. We still go to lectures and self-study, but the PBL sessions help us to remember and discuss the subjects with our peers. It isn't for everybody, though—I know a few people who switched schools because of it. The curriculum is also very intense. There is a lot to learn for each course, which takes place over a period of two to three months. I am doing a double major and just fit in all my required classes, but I cannot fail any or else I have to take a fourth year. Despite how intense it is, the experience has been amazing and I completely love the school.

— Lexi, age 20, from Orange County, CA, studying neuroscience and psychology at EUC

Admissions:

Intake: Fall

Application Period: October-January or April (depending on the program)

Admissions Decision Issued: Applications are evaluated as they are received and admissions decisions are issued shortly thereafter.

Diploma Equivalence: American high school applicants need four AP scores of 3+ for International Business, and Erasmus University College. If graduating with a diploma other than an EB, IB, American High School, or British A levels, check the nuffic site (nuffic.nl) for VWO equivalence under the overview of foreign diplomas.

SAT/ACT: Scores can be substituted for the math requirement for Erasmus University College or Communication and Media. SAT must be 1170 with math of 570; ACT must be 27 total with math sub score of 27.

Entrance Exam: All programs except Arts and Culture, History, Psychology, and Management of International Social Challenges have a math requirement that can be met through an entrance exam, AP calculus, or in some cases, ACT/SAT scores.

Other: American students require a GPA of 3.0 for International Business and Liberal Arts, 2.5 for Psychology and Management of International Social Challenges.

English Proficiency: Non-native speakers without an IB diploma must demonstrate proficiency.

TOEFL: 90 with sub-scores of at least 20
IELTS: 6.5 with no sub-score lower than 6
CAE: A-C
Scholarships: Non-EU students can apply for the 5,000-euro Holland Scholarship for their first year of study. Erasmus also has a relationship with Sallie Mae, which opens up the option of student loans for American students.

English-taught bachelor's degree programs:

Arts and Culture Studies	3 years	6,400 euros ($7,871.04) per year
Communication and Media	3 years	6,900 euros ($7,871.04) per year
Econometrics and Operations Research	3 years	9,000 euros ($11,068.65) per year
*Economics and Business Economics	3 years	9,000 euros ($11,068.65) per year
Econometrics and Economics	4 years	9,000 euros ($11,068.65) per year

History	3 years	6,900 euros ($7,871.04) per year
*Psychology	3 years	6,400 euros ($7,871.04) per year
*Business Administration	3 years	9,000 euros ($11,068.65) per year
*Management of International Social Challenges	3 years	6,400 euros ($7,871.04) per year
*Nanobiology	3 years	10,834 euros ($13,324) per year
*Liberal Arts and Sciences	(EUC) 3 years	12,000 euros ($14,817) per year

Majors

- Economics
- Business
- Economics, Business, and Society
- Philosophy, Politics, and Economics
- Humanities
- Political Philosophy &Critical Theory
- Visual Culture and Media Literacy

- Cultural Analysis
- Art, Culture and Society
- Life Science
- Pre-Med
- Neuroscience
- Molecular and Cellular Biology
- Global Health
- Biological Aspects of Public Health
- Social and Behavioral Sciences
- Psychology
- International Relations and Political Sciences
- Sociology and Urban Studies
- International Law

* Selective admissions procedure

Chapter Fifteen

Groningen University

Location: Groningen, Netherlands

Number of English-taught bachelors: 35

Average annual tuition: $11,727 (excluding medicine)

Duration: 3 years

Average tuition for full degree: $35,191

Groningen

A lot of people (including myself until recently) would have trouble naming cities in the Netherlands other than Amsterdam and maybe The Hague. But overlooking some of the lesser-known cities means potentially missing out on some great opportunities. Groningen is one such city that has a tremendous amount to offer students. Groningen is located in the northernmost part of the country, about a two-hour train ride from Amsterdam. It is the youngest city in the Netherlands, with half of the population under thirty-five. Further, 25% of the residents are students. Because Groningen is the main urban city in this part of the county and it has such a large student population, it is a haven of diverse culture with numerous museums, a thriving underground music scene, and many nightlife offerings geared toward students.

As is the case for many European schools, there is no true campus, and the school's buildings are located throughout the city. In some cities, this can seem disjointed, but in Groningen, it feels as though the city and the University are very connected, with the town serving as one big campus. Though it's a city with a population of more than 200,000, it definitely retains a small-town, community-minded feel. When I was there, I frequently observed people running into others they knew.

Groningen is the most bike-friendly city in the Netherlands and in the top five in all of Europe. This is due in large part because of a change in city infrastructure in the 1970s. Automobiles were on the rise in Groningen at that point, and the solution for the increasingly crowded roads was to build more roads, which often meant demolishing entire neighborhoods. Such plans did not sit well with everyone, though, and when twenty-four-year-old Max van den Berg found himself in charge of Groningen's traffic and urban development policy, he put forth what at the time seemed like an entirely radical idea: get rid of cars entirely and make the city center a safe space for cyclists and pedestrians.

While van den Berg's dream might not be entirely realized, it was in large part successful. It is impossible now to get directly from one point of Groningen to another—if you are in a car. Those walking or on bike though, have easy, direct access to anywhere they want to go, thereby making travel by car a time-consuming affair. Now, 60% of all traffic is bike traffic, and Groningen has the cleanest air of the larger Dutch cities. The city's dedication to remaining as bike-friendly as possible continues—plans are currently in the works for traffic lights that give cyclists priority when it's raining, heated bike paths to prevent slipping in colder weather, and more bike parking and more bike rentals.

I always felt like a bit of an outsider in the US, so I was ecstatic about coming to study in Europe. It's been all that I hoped for and more. The University is incredibly international and everyone has a different perspective and is not afraid to discuss and debate them. It was beyond refreshing to come to such an open-minded environment, especially given what is going on in the US currently. My two favorite things are the market and picnic season: the endless availability of cheap, fresh food—and flowers!—is a godsend and the summer picnics at *Noorderplantsoen* and *Hoornsemeer* are what dreams are made of. I've recommended the University and the whole European experience to every American who'd listen.

— Mareike, age 20, from Wilmington DE, studying English Language and Culture at UG

Living in Groningen

Other than the University College students who are required to live together the first year, University of Groningen students are responsible for locating their own housing. There are

2,000 rooms in the student residences reserved for international students, with many reserved specifically for those going to University of Groningen. Prices range from $425 – 675 (344.72 – 547.49 euros) per month in the student residences. Another alternative is getting a room in the Student Hotel, which, at $1,000 (811.10 euros) per month is more expensive than living in a student residence but offers amenities and options that international students might find useful. Rent includes a bike rental, weekly cleaning services, and add-on options for a meal plan. After the first year, many students end up renting apartments together, and roommates certainly help offset the monthly rent. Some students really look outside the box and get creative with their housing options, like the one I met who rented a houseboat!

University of Groningen

Founded in 1614, the University of Groningen (UG) is one of the oldest universities in Europe. Twenty percent of the school's 28,000 enrollments are international students, representing 120 different countries. The school offers thirty-five English-taught bachelor's degree programs, which is more than any other European college. Programs are offered in the arts, economics, and business (which have EQUIS and AACSB accreditation), behavioral and social sciences, theology and religious studies, medical sciences, law, spatial sciences, philosophy, science, and engineering. There are also two different university college options, with one in Groningen and the new Global Responsibility and Leadership University College in Fryslân.

Not only does Groningen offer a range of program options,

but most of them are interdisciplinary in nature. The Religious Studies program, for example, is not just focused on theology, but also includes psychology, sociology, anthropology, and philosophy. International and European Law students explore political science, economics, and international relations. The European Languages and Culture program includes European history, literature, language, society, and politics. Even some of the science and engineering programs are interdisciplinary, such as the Industrial Engineering program, which includes business and technology, or the Life Science and Technology program, with courses covering biology, pharmacy, physics, chemistry, and engineering.

Even programs with a more singular focus have options to broaden the scope. This can be done by adding a minor or participating in the honors program. Those who choose this route will take courses outside of their discipline, courses that are specifically created for honors program students. Further, some of these courses are within their main study area, which deepen their knowledge in their discipline.

All students have the option of adding a philosophy degree to their studies. Those who choose to do this generally spread the course requirements throughout their years of study, which enables them to graduate with only one extra year. After studying topics like the history of philosophy, logic, ethics, and political philosophy, students focus on philosophy as it pertains to their main area of study. This option is rare in the Netherlands and offered only at the University of Groningen and Erasmus University Rotterdam. Further, though Dutch is not required for academics and there is extremely high English proficiency throughout the city, international students are offered fifty hours of Dutch language classes at no cost. All programs have study advisors who can discuss these options with students, in addition to assisting with study skills, personal issues, and post-graduation plans.

Classes have a lecture component, but the same class also has a seminar and/or lab component. These are usually limited to ten to fifteen students and attendance is mandatory. As with all schools in the Netherlands, students are encouraged—and expected—to disagree with the professor during group discussions. In order to do this, students must come prepared to each class. At the beginning of the nine-week block, students receive a schedule that communicates what will be taught each week, along with the expected reading throughout the week to prepare for the lecture and seminar group. This is not checked on through assignments, but will determine success for the tests, participation grades, presentations, and projects.

Some Americans wonder if going to college in Europe means having to forfeit the typical social experience one would have at a school in the United States. Groningen offers the social experiences one would have in the United States—just packaged differently. Each academic department at Groningen has a main study association for the students in all the programs within that department. Many have more specific program associations as well, but the main activity occurs at the department level. For instance, the Economics and Business Faculty Association (EBF) is the main study association for all students taking programs in the Economics and Business Department. There are also more specific associations within the department, like the Marketing Association (MARUG), Financial Study Association (RISK), Study Association for

Econometrics and Operations Research (Vesting), and the Study Association for Technology Management (TEMA). EBF offers events pertaining to study, career, and social life. Study events include leadership panels, economic and business conferences, and symposiums related to the departmental fields of study. Social events include monthly get-togethers, holiday balls, weekend trips, and beer tastings.

Most of the university-level career centers in the Netherlands provide workshops and services around the skills and tools needed to get a job, but the important recruitment and networking opportunities occur through the departmental study associations. EBF, for instance, has traditional recruitment days in addition to less conventional networking events. A great example of this is the networking pub quiz event featuring EY consultants from four different departments. There is also the Consultancy Tour in which twenty-five selected students visit five major companies, work on a case to get a taste of life as a consultant, and attend informal networking events. Groningen is a hot spot for fast-growing start-ups and innovation, so it's not surprising that EBF also offers a series of Entrepreneurship Evenings.

Orientation events for new students are provided at the program, university and city level. The school and program activities introduce students to the University-wide resources, program logistics, and involve plenty of parties and opportunities to socialize with the other new students. ESN provides an orientation week for international students, which includes tours of the city, sports, parties, Dutch language classes, and dinners. KEI is an organization that functions to introduce all new students (international and Dutch, from both universities in the city) to Groningen. Each year, 5,000 new students participate in KEI events, which are led by seasoned students. These events and activities are purely social in nature, providing parties, dinners, pub-crawls, and events introducing students to the various student societies and sports opportunities. The program also includes workshops around making mature student life choices, like being a good neighbor, looking out for each other in social situations, and making smart choices about sexual activity, drugs, and alcohol.

The opportunities to get involved are almost endless at the UG. In addition to the societies and groups offered at the program level, the University has a number of choices, such as the student orchestra, cabaret, band, concert choir, acapella troupe, and English-based theater society. There are also political groups, associations for students from a specific country or region, and others for all international students. There is no lack of sports opportunities either! The ACLO is the sports organization for both University of Groningen and the university of applied science in the city, Hanze. It is the biggest sports center in the Netherlands, offering forty-nine different sports clubs to the 19,000 student members for less than $75 (60.83 euros) per year!

In brief:

Students who don't want to miss out on the traditional US student life experience should consider Groningen. Though it might not be as well-known as Amsterdam or The Hague, this super bike-friendly city is paradise for students. And with the most English-taught bachelor's degree programs out of any school in Europe, Groningen is worth consideration even if student life is less of an important factor.

Admissions:

Intake: Fall

Application Period: October – May 1ˢᵗ

Admission Decision Issued: Rolling admissions with decisions provided within 4-6 weeks.

Diploma Equivalence: American students require an IB diploma or four AP scores of 3+. If graduating with a diploma other than an EB, IB, American High School, or British A levels, check the nuffic site (nuffic.nl) for VWO equivalence under the overview of foreign diplomas.

SAT/ACT: No

Entrance Exam: Certain programs have math requirements that can be demonstrated by higher level math courses (e.g., AP or HL) or a math exam held throughout the year in Utrecht.

English Proficiency: Non-native speakers without an IB diploma must demonstrate proficiency.

TOEFL: 92

IELTS: 6.5

Scholarships: Non-EU students can apply for the 5,000 euro ($6,149.25) Holland Scholarship for their first year of study. Groningen also has a number with Sallie Mae, which opens up the option for student loans for American students.

English-taught bachelor's degree programs:

American Studies	3 years	8,300 euros ($10,207.76) per year
Art History	3 years	8,300 euros ($10,207.76) per year
Arts, Culture, and Media	3 years	8,300 euros ($10,207.76) per year
Communication and Information Studies	3 years	8,300 euros ($10,207.76) per year
English Language and Culture	3 years	8,300 euros ($10,207.76) per year
European Languages and Cultures	3 years	8,300 euros ($10,207.76) per year
History	3 years	8,300 euros ($10,207.76) per year
*International Relations and International Organizations	3 years	8,300 euros ($10,207.76) per year

Media Studies	3 years	8,300 euros ($10,207.76) per year
Minorities and Multilingualism	3 years	8,300 euros ($10,207.76) per year
Econometrics and Operations Research	3 years	8,300 euros ($10,207.76) per year
Economics and Business Economics	3 years	8,300 euros ($10,207.76) per year
International Business	3 years	8,300 euros ($10,207.76) per year
Applied Mathematics	3 years	10,900 euros ($13,405.37) per year
Applied Physics	3 years	10,900 euros ($13,405.37) per year
Artificial Intelligence	3 years	10,900 euros ($13,405.37) per year
Astronomy	3 years	10,900 euros ($13,405.37) per year

Biology	3 years	10,900 euros ($13,405.37) per year
Chemical Engineering	3 years	10,900 euros ($13,405.37) per year
Chemistry	3 years	10,900 euros ($13,405.37) per year
Computing Science	3 years	10,900 euros ($13,405.37) per year
Industrial Engineering and Management	3 years	10,900 euros ($13,405.37) per year
Life Science and Technology	3 years	10,900 euros ($13,405.37) per year
Mathematics	3 years	10,900 euros ($13,405.37) per year
Pharmacy	3 years	10,900 euros ($13,405.37) per year
Physics	3 years	10,900 euros ($13,405.37) per year

*Global Health	3 years	32,000 euros ($39,355.20) per year
*Molecular Medicine	3 years	32,000 euros ($39,355.20) per year
Human Geography and Urban and Regional Planning	3 years	8,300 euros ($10,207.56) per year
Spatial Planning and Design	3 years	8,300 euros ($10,207.56) per year
Psychology	3 years	8,300 euros ($10,207.56) per year
International and European Law	3 years	8,300 euros ($10,207.56) per year
Religious Studies	3 years	8,300 euros ($10,207.56) per year
*Global Responsibility and Leadership (University College)	3 years	12,100 euros ($14,881.19) per year
*Liberal Arts and Sciences (University College)	3 years	12,000 euros ($14,758.20) per year

Majors:

- Health and Life Sciences
- Physics of Energy
- Brain, Behavior, and Culture
- Philosophy, Politics, and International law
- Philosophy, Politics, and Economics
- Humanities
- Journalism, Media, and History
- The Arts
- Culture Studies
- Philosophy

Part Four: The Most Expensive Schools Are Still a Bargain!

Students who expand their search beyond in-state public schools in the United States will pay an average of $34,740 a year for private universities, and $25,620 for out-of-state public universities (with an average of $30,180 between the two). The schools in this section might be more expensive than many other schools in Europe, but still cost at least 50% less than the total tuition a student would pay at an out-of-state or private US university.

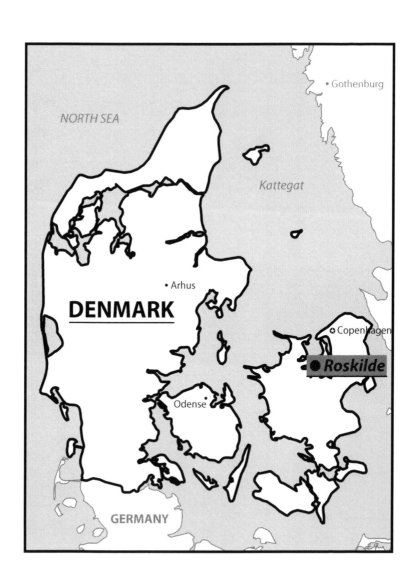

Chapter Sixteen
Roskilde University

Location: Roskilde, Denmark

Number of English-taught bachelors: 3

Average annual tuition: $14,425

Duration: 3 years

Average tuition for full degree: $43,275

Denmark

Renowned for its high quality of life and often-voted the "happiest country in the world," Denmark is a popular study destination that offers its students a world-class education. It is also one of Europe's safest countries, and its residents enjoy high levels of equality and freedom of speech.

Situated in Northern Europe, Denmark is a small country with a population of 5.5 million. It is bordered by Germany to the south and is connected in the east to Sweden by the five-mile long Øresundsbroen Bridge. The Scandinavian countries are all generally associated with winter, though Denmark does not get quite as cold as its neighbors. In winter, the temperature averages in the thirties and the shortest day is six hours. By summer, the weather is pleasant, with temperatures into the high sixties. *Hygge* is a Danish concept that has received a lot of international attention and certainly helps make the short winter days more enjoyable. It's an untranslatable word, but speaks to contentment with simple pleasures and coziness. Of course, this is not exclusive to winter, but you can feel concrete signs of it on the cold and dark days, whether it's curling up with a cozy blanket and a book, the candlelight in the windows of cafés, or sitting around a fire with a group of friends. *Hygge* is about enjoying the moment, however simple.

Like the Netherlands, Denmark is known for its world-class cycling. Denmark's capital, Copenhagen, regularly tops lists as the world's most bike-friendly city and the best city for cyclists. A love for bikes extends throughout the entire country, and Danes do not let snow deter them from their bikes. Denmark boasts almost 7,000 miles of marked bike routes, and many of them are dedicated cycle paths.

The education system of Denmark is excellent and benefits from a large amount of government expenditure. Around 80% of the population speaks English, and 60% of Danes have a higher education. Perhaps even more impressive is that the adult literacy rate is at 99%. Like other Scandinavian countries, there is a distinct flat hierarchy between teachers and students. Students address their professors by their first names and are expected to actively participate in class discussions. Students are encouraged to disagree with the professor during these discussions, as individuality is valued as much as equality.

At the end of the school week, a bar is set up in each academic department, dubbed "Friday bars." Students within the department then have a place and time to socialize with other students, as well as their professors. There are two things striking about this: One is how informal and accessible the student-teacher relationship is, particularly in comparison to US schools. The other thing this highlights is the different attitude to drinking in Europe. The drinking culture amongst students in Europe does not happen exclusively in the context of "partying" as is often the case in the United States.

Roskilde

Roskilde is part of the Greater Copenhagen area, located a quick twenty-minute train ride away from the capital city. Around 50,000 people live here, with more than 15% of them being students. The city is the tenth largest in Denmark and is one of the country's oldest cities.

Roskilde is also home to Roskilde Cathedral, a UNESCO World Heritage Site. Constructed during the 12th and 13th centuries, this Gothic cathedral was the first of its kind to be built with bricks and began the Brick Gothic style that is commonly seen throughout Northern Europe. Denmark also has a rich Viking heritage, which can be explored at the Viking Ship Museum. Visitors can see five original Viking ships that had been deliberately sunk all the way back in 1070.

Music is very important here. Since 1971, Roskilde has hosted the Roskilde Festival, an annual multi-day music fest. What originally started as a small, Woodstock-inspired off-shoot meant to celebrate the music of the 1960s, has since grown into the largest music festival in Northern Europe. Think Lollapalooza but bigger and longer, with more than 175 acts, and more than 150,000 attendees—three times the city's population! There is also the "Ragnarock Museum for pop, rock, and youth culture" that explores the history of music from the 1950s all the way up to today's present-day pop and beyond.

For those looking to spend time in the natural world, Roskilde's national park, Skjoldungernes Land, provides ample opportunity to explore a stunning Ice Age landscape. Roskilde Fjord is another place where you will find an abundance of natural beauty, as well as evidence of human activity dating all the way back to the Stone Ages.

Living in Roskilde

Housing is difficult for students throughout Denmark, and Roskilde is no exception. Housing can be found, but do expect headaches. Though Roskilde is less expensive than Copenhagen, Denmark as a whole is an expensive country. Expect to spend anywhere from $500 – 850 (406.55 – 691.14 euros) per month for housing, though savings can be found by sharing an apartment with other students.

Getting around Roskilde is relatively easy, thanks to its great public transportation system. In fact, within the city proper, the majority of residents live less than a third of a mile from the nearest bus station or train stop. Students are eligible to apply for public transportation discounts including the DSB Ung card. It costs around $20 (125 DKK) annually and provides a discount of up to 50% on travel within Denmark.

Roskilde University

Roskilde University (RUC) was founded in 1972 as an alternative to traditional education in Denmark. It was developed to give students a voice in their education and use innovative and creative teaching methods. Denmark has since adopted similar educational philosophies and approaches, but Roskilde is progressive amongst progressives. They now educate more than 9,000 students, 10% international, from 90 countries, and are known for their interdisciplinary, problem-based project work emphasis.

RUC offers three different English-taught bachelor's degree programs: Humanities, Social Sciences, and Natural Sciences. Their programs are uniquely structured. During the first year, students study courses related to their field. For instance, students in the Social Sciences program take political science, sociology, economics, and research-focused classes, such as qualitative and quantitative methods. Students in the Humanities and Natural Science programs also take the research-focused classes, in addition to broad classes related to their field of study.

The second year opens up a number of interesting options as students choose two subject areas of focus, and one can be outside of their program area. The subject area choices are:

- Communication studies
- Cultural encounters
- Psychology
- Business administration

- Business studies
- International studies
- Chemistry
- Computer science
- Environmental biology
- Mathematics
- Molecular biology
- Physics

Certainly, the options for combining fields open up a number of possibilities. A psychology student, for instance, could combine their studies with business, communication, international studies, or cultural encounters, providing a different context and framework for each subject. A computer science student can integrate their subject with business, chemistry, communication, environmental biology, mathematics, molecular biology, or physics. These combinations affect the lens in which you view the subject matter, and can be tailored to fit a particular interest. There are defined options for course combinations so that the University can ensure they are integrated in a relevant and coherent manner.

Not only does RUC give its students the freedom to choose subjects of interest, but they have unique, interdisciplinary way to make these subjects and their combinations meaningful. This is achieved through their project- and problem-based learning. Each semester, students take two courses and one project. The project itself is worth 15 ECTS (half of the total semester credits). The beginning phase of the project is organized and structured, starting with a broad topic. Over a period of about two to three days, an academic committee helps students form smaller groups of about three to six, based on their academic interests. Once the students decide on their research question, they are assigned a supervisor, who regularly meets with the group to provide guidance. The report is submitted at the end of the semester, along with an oral report, and students are provided individual grades. The projects during the first three semesters are related to their program, (e.g., Humanities) while the fourth and fifth semesters pertain to their chosen specialty subjects.

The groups start by identifying a research question. In the past, students in the Social Science program have focused on the role recent disfranchisement of the Sunnis played in ISIS's rise to power and how digital activism challenges political systems. Humanities students have looked at how well-educated people from different cultures react to media exposure on homosexuality and how mixed heritage people negotiate their cultures in defining their identity in Danish society. Natural Science students explore how thermal conductivity and heat capacity of the stack material influence the thermoacoustic effect and to what extent miRNAs play a role in breast cancer.

The two classes students take each semester provide them with the knowledge, theories, and tools that are then applied to the project work. Teachers are there to teach students how to learn and what questions to ask; not to teach a fixed view on things. Professors aren't facilitators of knowledge, but facilitators of learning and problem-solving. Because students determine their own research question and focus area around their academic interests, the work becomes more meaningful. Further, students often collaborate with organizations and companies in both the public and private sector as part of their project, which provides exposure to different fields and networking opportunities. This type of fieldwork equips students with important skills, such as conducting research, collaboration, and analytics. Because fieldwork is a component of every semester, students have ample opportunity to practice these skills, which will only serve them well when it comes time to apply what they have learned in real-life job situations.

RUC is a centralized campus with modern, state-of-the-art facilities. Communication students have access to video editing equipment, image processing and payout programs, video cameras, and a large cinema. The Natural Science department has various equipment and computers with specialized software and technical support. The University's library is both a research and a public library, and serves as a welcoming workspace for students and teachers alike. The campus also features a canteen, where food is priced based on weight. Expect to pay anywhere from $3.25 – 6.50 (2.64 – 5.29 euros) for a meal, with sandwiches averaging around $4 (3.25 euros).

RUC provides its students with a vast array of resources pertaining to academics, social life, and employment after graduation. Access to many of these resources can be found through the Student Hub, where students can get help choosing classes, information about study abroad, and counseling and career assistance. Of particular interest are the career-service offerings geared toward international students. RUC participates in a program that helps international students learn about and gain access to the Danish job market upon graduating through presentations, conferences, networking events, and job portals. As one of the few European countries that is close to full employment, there is a definite labor shortage in Denmark. Companies want to hire people, yet there are often not enough skilled residents, particularly in the IT, computer science, and engineering fields. International students can benefit greatly from this labor shortage, as companies in Denmark are eager to hire qualified workers.

Each student is part of a "house" based on their study area. The different houses offer students various social and academic resources and opportunities. They arrange for relevant guest lecturers, company visits, and academic-related excursions, such as mushroom gathering, for students in environmental biology. Each house has a social committee that arrange parties, Friday bars, barbecues, and holiday events. The building itself has a kitchen, group study rooms, and computers, and also serves to help integrate students into the daily (and social) life of the department.

Just as study is not confined to one discipline, socialization opportunities are not restricted to one's study house either. The Student House is RUC's inclusive gathering space, with plenty of lounge and study areas for students. It also houses the RUC café and bar is run by students and hosts a number of social events throughout the year. There are a number of additional ways to get involved through student associations, the student council, and Kamarillaen, which is the group that organizes the huge annual RUC party.

Students are first introduced to social life on campus (as well as academic information and resources) through the two-week orientation before the start of the first year. There is also a mentor program to help international students acclimate to the school, city, and student-life opportunities. The University has a strong International Club, which offers trips, parties, holiday celebrations, and more. In the past, they have hosted a *Stranger Things* marathon, a canal tour, pub quizzes, jam sessions, and cooking events with cultural themes. There is no shortage of unique, community-building events at RUC.

In brief:

Roskilde University's unique structuring of its academics allows students to combine areas of study, thus creating a program tailored specifically to each student's individual interests. Despite its higher tuition and the difficulty one might encounter in finding housing in Denmark, RUC is an excellent choice for those looking for project-based learning in one of the happiest countries in the world.

Admissions:

Intake: Fall

Application Period: February – March 15th

Admission Decision Issued: By June 1st

Diploma Equivalence: IB diploma, American high school diploma with three AP scores of 3+ or one year of college credits, European Baccalaureate, British A-levels.

Specific country requirements can be found at *www.ufm.dk/en*, following the links to the international qualification for entry to undergraduate programs.

SAT/ACT: No

Entrance Exam: No

Other: The Danish application is called the Coordinated Enrollment System or "KOT." Students can apply at up to eight programs or apply for all the schools in the country. You rank the schools in order of preference when you apply. If you qualify for more than one, you get your highest choice pick. You won't be accepted at more than one.

RUC international applicants who meet the admissions qualifications are ranked according to their academic background, motivation, and relevant experience.

The Humanities program requires that applicants have Arabic, Chinese, French, German, Greek, Italian, Japanese, Latin, Russian, Spanish, or Turkish at the Danish A level or German, French, or Danish at the Danish B-level. Other programs have math, science, or history requirements in Danish A or B levels. These correspond to the hours of instruction in the course over the past three years. A-levels are equivalent to 325-375 instruction hours and B levels require 130 – 210, depending on the subject.

English Proficiency: Roskilde does not accept English tests. Applicants must document the hours of English instruction for the Danish B-level (210 hours).

Scholarships: No

English-taught bachelor's programs:

Humanities	3 years	8,700 euros ($10,699.70) per year
Natural Sciences	3 years	18,000 euros ($22,137.30) per year
Social Sciences	3 years	8,700 euros ($10,699.70) per year

Chapter Seventeen

Vesalius College

> Location: Brussels, Belgium
> Number of English-taught bachelor's: 4
> Average annual tuition: $14,550
> Duration: 3 years
> Average tuition for full degree: $43,650

Belgium

Belgium is one of the smallest and most densely populated countries in the EU, with 11.35 million people. For such a relatively small nation, the country is unique in having three official languages—Flemish (or Belgian Dutch), French, and German. Flemish is spoken in the Flanders area in the North, while the Wallonia region of the South is predominantly French speaking. To the east, you will find the German-speaking community of Belgium, where approximately 77,000 people speak German. Though not an official language, English is also spoken widely, especially in the capital city, Brussels. Belgium is bordered by France, Luxembourg, Germany, and the Netherlands. A small portion of its northwest border sits on the North Sea and is home to some truly pristine beaches.

There are several airports in Belgium, with Brussels Airport being the main one. Despite its name, this airport is actually located in Flanders and offers flights from full-service carriers as well as a number of budget carriers. Belgium has an excellent integrated public transportation system, which makes getting around very easy. A MOBIB-card can be purchased for five euros ($6.14) and can be used to load any type of travel or pass.

Brussels

Brussels, known as the "Heart of Europe" is a truly cosmopolitan city with 31% of its residents being foreign. The city is headquarters not just to the EU but also NATO, making it a major center for international politics. It holds the world's largest press corps, as well as hundreds of NGOs and multinational corporations.

The location makes other world-class cities, such as Paris, London, and Amsterdam, easily accessible in less than two hours by train. For those who want to escape the city, the beaches of the North are reachable in slightly more than an hour and the public transportation system is easy to use, making it ideal for exploring other great Belgian cities such as Antwerp (the diamond capital of Europe) and the medieval city of Bruges.

Sadly, many people first think of the 2016 terrorist attack when hearing about Brussels, and, thus, question the safety of the city. I have discussed this issue with American students who live in Brussels, and they all had interesting perspectives. They noted that terrorism has happened in many cities, including those in American cities, like Boston, New York, and

Orlando. We discussed how horrible events can create a new normal of sorts, such as here in the United States where there are regular lockdown drills in elementary schools to prepare students for the possibility of an active shooter. There is now a strong police and military presence in Brussels, which has increased since the 2016 attack. This example of the "new normal" in Brussels further contributes to their sense of safety.

Living in Brussels

Vesalius College (VeCo) is located twenty minutes from the city center. The school provides assistance in locating housing and students can stay in residences throughout the city. Rooms in the student residences can be found for $550 – 675 (450-550 euros) per month. Bikes are available to rent for $40 (33 euros) per semester and a student metro pass costs $61 (50 euros) for the year.

Vesalius College

VeCo was founded in 1987 by Vrije University Brussels and Boston University, to provide English-taught bachelor's pro-grams that merged what they viewed as the best parts of both the European and American approaches to education. To this end, they developed and implemented "Theory-Guided, Practice-Embedded and Experiential Learning," or TPEL. The idea behind this approach is that with a pure research focus, you don't know how to apply what you have learned; with focus on only practice, you don't have the theory that allows you to generalize your knowledge and apply it elsewhere.

The deliberate merging of these two philosophies teaches students how to apply the theories to real-life situations, which makes learning relevant and leads to critical thinking. Critical thinking is key in TPEL, so much so that all students in bachelor's degree programs are required to take a course on it. Further, critical thought often develops through exposure to a variety of perspectives, and VeCo has students who come from sixty different countries. Combined with the interactive teaching style, small classes, and group work, students are exposed first-hand to perspectives from around the world, which is crucial for critical thought development. Such an approach prepares students with both the theoretical knowledge and hands-on experience they need in order to succeed post-graduation.

All of the degree programs are conducted in English, with bachelor's programs offered in Global Business and Entrepreneurship, International and European Law, Global Communication, and International Affairs. Because TPEL is unique, it is helpful to look at how it is implemented in a specific program, namely International Affairs.

Theoretical knowledge occurs throughout most of the courses, which include relevant and timely classes like Legal Aspects of Migration, NATO and Transatlantic Approaches to Security, and Global Terrorism, Counter Terrorism and De-Radicalization. For the practice and experiential components, International Affairs students benefit from the school's location in Brussels. The school has guest lecturers that include speakers from NATO, the UN, various relevant EU committee chairs and directors, ambassadors, and foreign ministers. Students must participate in a capstone project, which involves working with high-ranking diplomats on foreign policy issues. They also have the option of doing internships for academic credit. VeCo also has an impressive list of sixty different internship partners, which include organizations such as EY Belgium, NATO Headquarters, United Nations, various embassies, Time Warner, UPS, ING, and the European Parliament.

Students in all of the programs take core classes in academic writing, critical thinking, global ethics, statistics, leadership and personal development, and research methods. A minor may be declared in:

- Digital Economy
- Family Business
- International Management and Governance
- Marketing
- Media Studies
- Strategic Communication
- European Peace and Security Studies
- EU studies
- Global Governance
- History
- Business Law
- European Law
- International Law

Unlike many other Belgian schools, which base grades almost solely on final exams, courses at Vesalius are continuously assessed through projects, papers, and exams. Further, the fall semester ends before the winter break, so students don't have to spend their holiday studying for finals.

The student body at VeCo consists of only 350 students. This, of course, causes initial concerns for many people. They worry that a school this size would be limited in their resources related to academic or student life. That is not the case here. The immense Vrije University Brussels (VUB) campus is right across the street from VeCo. Though VeCo has its own private school status and functions independently, the relationship between the schools allows all VeCo students access to the Vesalius facilities: a library, student associations, sports facilities—that offer more than thirty sports—fitness equipment and classes, an indoor swimming pool, a track, tennis courts, squash, rock climbing, soccer, and more. VeCo students can dine at the cafeteria, which sources many of its ingredients from organic farms and won the SMC Sustainable Seafood Certificate in 2013. In addition to the access to the various facilities, VeCo students can also take classes at Vesalius.

VeCo's small size actually comes with some great benefits. One such benefit is the personalized attention and community feel fostered by the student body at VeCo. The small size allows the students to really get to know each other and the professors. The community feel is almost tangible, and was easily observed while I spent time in a student lounge area.

The school offers many opportunities for student life. The Vesalius Student Government (VSG) is made up of elected students who take on an active role as liaison between students and the academic administration. The VSG also organizes a number of different activities, including sports, parties, clubs, midterm and finals parties, winter ball, potlucks, tutoring, student focus groups, cinema club and volunteer clubs. The VSG also assists with the mandatory three-day orientation that hosts a variety of social events and provides new students with information about social life and academic life.

Each student is assigned a professor who acts as an advisor, as well as a separate career advisor, which speaks to the priority of educating students and also making them employable. Eighty percent of bachelor's students go on for a master's degree at schools such as Georgetown, London School of Economics, Boston University, Bocconi University, Columbia, Brown, and University of Edinburgh. Post-graduation, students have found employment at various think tanks, embassies, and large corporations such as Facebook.

In brief:

VeCo provides its students with a close-knit, boutique education with all the resources and infrastructure of large research universities—in essence, the best of both worlds. While at first glance some might be inclined to think the small size would limit what is both available and achievable, Vesalius students actually have many advantages when they attend this school in the heart of Europe.

Admissions:

Intake: Fall and Spring

Application Period: Rolling admissions is used. Non-EU students should apply by May 31st for Fall and November 30th for Spring.

Admission Decision Issued: 3 weeks after completed application is received.

Diploma Equivalence: IB diploma, American high school diploma, European Baccalaureate, or a secondary education that provides eligibility for higher education in your home country. This includes a school certificate and national exams, if applicable.

SAT/ACT: Evidence-Based Reading & Writing 550/800, SAT Math 550/800 for American students.

English Proficiency: Non-native speakers must prove English proficiency
TOEFL: 90
IELTS: 6.5

Scholarships: Academic Excellence Scholarship is awarded as a tuition waiver of up to 50%. Students need 3.8 GPA and minimum ACT of 29 or 1260 SAT. This scholarship is renewed so long as performance is maintained.

English-taught bachelor's degree programs:

Global Business, and Entrepreneurship	3 years	11,800 euros ($14,496.30) per year
Global Communication	3 years	11,800 euros ($14,496.30) per year
International Affairs	3 years	11,800 euros ($14,496.30) per year
International and European Law	3 years	11,800 euros ($14,496.30) per year

Chapter Seventeen

Bocconi University

Location: Milan, Italy

Number of English-taught bachelors: 7

Average annual tuition: $17,357

Duration: 3 years

Average tuition for full program: $52,071

Italy

With its impressive historical heritage, popular cuisine, friendly people, and beautiful landscape, it is easy to see why many students are drawn to Italy. The country boasts more UNESCO World Heritage Sites than any other country and is also home to the oldest university in the world: the University of Bologna.

Italy is bordered by France to the northwest, Switzerland and Austria to the north, and Slovenia to the northeast. It is the fourth most populous country in the EU, with the eighth largest economy in the world. Although a relatively small country, the weather here varies considerably from north to south. For example, in the mountainous alpine areas of the north temperatures can be cold enough for snow during winter, making it a popular skiing area, while to the south, temperatures rarely drop below the 40s.

More than any other country I visited, I was struck by the differences between the public and private universities in Italy. The public universities charge tuition based on family income. This applies to all students, including international students, with a maximum tuition at most schools of less than $5,000 (4,000 euros) per year. While the price is enticing, the facilities of the public schools I visited were quite basic, and large lectures are customary. There are fewer services directed toward students' growth and development, as the main priority at these schools is purely academic. Certainly the trade-offs are worth it for some, but not for all. I want to emphasize that this is not the case in most other countries, where in many instances, I was more impressed by the public universities than the private ones.

There are unique obstacles when applying to colleges in Italy. The first applies to master's and bachelor's degree students applying to both private and public universities. It is a headache called "pre-enrollment." This procedure was put in place in the days before the internet and has not changed with the times. First, a student applies to a school in Italy. The school then issues a pre-acceptance letter (or rejection). The student takes the pre-acceptance letter, along with a ton of other required documents, to the Italian embassy in their home country for pre-enrollment. This is what initiates the visa process. The student is officially enrolled once they are in Italy in the fall and turn in their documents to the school.

Sound complicated? It can be, but it can also get even trickier. Some undergraduate programs have an entrance exam. SAT and ACT scores can substitute for many of them, but not for all. For instance, all the medical programs require entrance exams, as do programs like architecture. Private universities tend to have their entrance exams in the spring and often offer them in cities around the world. Public universities generally hold theirs on campus in Italy in September. And by September, I mean a mere month before classes begin. From a planning perspective, this would personally make me really anxious!

Finally, the Italian government requires that American students have either an IB or three AP scores of 3+ to enroll in bachelor's programs. This is because Italian students have thirteen years of education, while we have twelve in the United States. A full year of college can substitute for the AP requirement and some schools allow three academic college courses to substitute. Word on the street is that the government is considering getting rid of the pre-enrollment process and looking at other ways to assess educational equivalence besides the APs. Fingers crossed!

Milan

I have always loved to visit Italy, but the northern areas feel much more livable and less touristy than the other places I have been. Right in the north of the country, near the Swiss border, is the city of Milan. It is the second most populated city in Italy, after Rome, and is well-known as being the design and fashion capital of Europe. Here you'll find a blend of historical and modern architecture throughout the city. The centerpiece is the Duomo di Milano Cathedral, which took almost six hundred years to complete. It is the third-largest church in the world, and the largest in Italy. Its façade is an impressive blend of the Baroque and Neo-Gothic, with massive spires, ornate carvings, and stained-glass windows.

Living in Milan

Milan is one of Italy's most cosmopolitan cities as residents hail from not just all over Italy but the whole world. The city has a lively nightlife with a plethora of popular bars and clubs throughout. Milan is also home to two big soccer (what is known as football throughout Europe) clubs, Inter Milan and AC Milan. At one point, both teams ranked at the top of the sport, but in more recent years have waned in success.

As the financial capital of Italy, Milan is one of the country's more expensive cities. It is a compact city and very easy to get around, both within the city and also getting elsewhere in Italy and Europe. I was able to get to Bologna and Turin in an hour by train. You can get to Lugano, Switzerland, in less than ninety minutes, and Rome in less than three hours. That said, the train travel is not inexpensive. My flights from Paris to Milan and Milan to Sofia were both less expensive than my train travel within the country. Fortunately, there are three airports in the region with many low-cost airlines.

The University of Bocconi is a ten-minute walk from the city center of Milan, but you will find much of what is needed on campus. Unlike many European schools, Bocconi has a centralized campus that even provides housing. They currently have seven student residences with an eighth opening the summer of 2018. Rooms are single occupancy and range from around $740 – 860 (600-700 euros) per month and include a weekly cleaning service.

University of Bocconi

The University of Bocconi was founded in 1902 and currently educates 13,876 students, 15% of whom are international. The majority of the programs here are taught in English and focus primarily on business and economics. The school holds triple crown accreditation, making it part of a small, elite group of business schools who hold this distinction.

Almost all of the programs are related to economics and management, with program options that integrate these subjects with social sciences, computer science, finance, arts, culture, communication, and more. In addition, there is a bachelor's degree in International Politics and Government. Bocconi also offers a four-year *World Business* Bachelor's degree program (WBB) where students have the opportunity to study at three renowned business schools, each located in a different major economic zone. The first year the students study at the University of Southern California Marshall School of Business in Los Angeles. The second year is spent at Hong Kong University of Science and Technology, and the third year is at Bocconi. They are able to choose where they go for their fourth year, and graduate with a full degree from all three universities.

Bachelor's students in all the other Bocconi programs take introductory courses in political economics, corporate economics, law, computer science, and quantitative methods. Bocconi recognizes that being able to interact effectively with others is crucial to their students' future success so they include soft skill and critical thinking seminars in the curriculum. The Counseling and Self-Empowerment office (which is a fantastic name) also assists with soft skills through workshops on public speaking, body language, goal setting, and time management.

The Bocconi campus is in the midst of major renovations. In addition to the student residence, they are building an updated rec center with an Olympic-size pool. Bocconi currently has a lacrosse team and a soccer team, as well as intramural and other options for track, hiking, judo, basketball, volleyball, boxing, rugby, skiing, snowboarding, sailing, and tennis. There are a number of student associations pertaining to various interests outside of academics and athletics, such as a student media center, which includes student radio, web TV, and a newspaper.

What really struck me about Bocconi is the international approach they take to education. This is something that is easy for schools to *say* they do, but Bocconi truly does practice what they preach. Traditionally, higher education in Italy has revolved around lectures, with little interaction between students or students and the professor. This is still the case at many public universities. At Bocconi however, the entering class is split into cohorts of no more than 100 students, so even the largest lecture will not feel overly crowded. The classroom layout is intentionally designed to be conducive to an interactive environment and the teaching methods include case studies, simulations, discussions, and group work. These different methods serve to enhance students' knowledge while at the same time providing skills in problem-solving and negotiating.

For the past fifteen years, every professor that has been hired at Bocconi is fluent in English and is either a non-Italian or an Italian who received their Ph.D in an international program university. This creates a diverse team of professors who are not resistant to an international educational model and approach. In addition to the guidance offered by professors, every program has directors to serve as resources to the students and each student has an academic advisor.

Though the campus environment is already quite international, with more than ninety nationalities represented, Bocconi sees the value of providing students opportunity for further international exposure throughout their studies. Students are required to learn two languages and can choose from French, Portuguese, Italian, Spanish, and German. They must gain B2 levels of proficiency in one and B1 in the other. Students are strongly encouraged to study abroad and it is mandatory for some of the programs.

Students at Bocconi have numerous opportunities for study both within the EU and outside of it. In addition to the Eramsus+ program, which provides students with study abroad options throughout Europe, Bocconi has 275 bilateral agreements with schools around the world. This means students can study outside the EU for no additional tuition fees. They have more than 50 partner schools in the United States including *Princeton, Columbia, Duke, Georgetown, NYU, Northwestern,* and *University of Chicago,* and equally impressive names throughout Latin America, Canada, Asia, Australia, New Zealand, and the Middle East.

Though the majority of students who graduate from the bachelor's degree programs go on for a master's degree, the job placement department has a dedicated team of more than seventy to help students with internships and job placements. Students who do not go on to get their master's find employment, on average, in 2.1 months. Almost half are employed abroad, with 13% working in the United States.

Career counselors help students identify their aptitudes, strengths, weaknesses, and interests, and use this information to guide plans for internships and employment. In addition to regular events and presentations throughout the year, Bocconi holds a job fair twice a year where students have access to more than 100 companies. Top recruiters include Accenture, Goldman Sachs, Google, L'Oreal, J.P. Morgan, Microsoft, Morgan Stanley, the United Nations, Deloitte, Ernst & Young, and many more!

In brief:

As I have mentioned many times before, it is crucial that we look at quality indicators beyond rankings, whether looking at schools in the United States or colleges abroad. We should seek a classroom environment that fosters interaction and cultivation of critical thought, international exposure, development of skills needed for employment, ample student supports, and outcomes pertaining to employment. Bocconi checks all of these boxes and more. Though it is more expensive than some of the schools in Europe, there is a very favorable probability of a high return on investment as it pertains to learning, employment, and personal growth.

Admissions:

Intake: Fall

Admissions Periods and Decision: Bocconi has three admissions rounds for undergraduate enrollment. The first round takes place in June of the year before studies begin (junior year for those in high school). These applicants are given an admission decision in September. The next round is in February, with decisions announced in March, and the third round is in April, with an admission decision in May. Students can apply to all three admissions rounds as they don't allocate all the spots to any one round.

Diploma Equivalence: American high school diploma with three AP scores of 3+ (Bocconi requires a fourth), IB diploma, or a secondary education that provides eligibility for higher education in your home country. This includes a school certificate and national exams, if applicable. The diplomas must be awarded after at least twelve years of studies and at least two full years of attendance must have been in the educational system issuing the diploma.

SAT/ACT: Yes. American students must submit minimum scores of 1300 for SAT or 29 for ACT. SAT subject score can substitute for the fourth AP test.

Entrance Exam: No

Other: Honors or AP course work in calculus, economics, stats, or computer science is recommended.

English Proficiency: Non-native speakers must submit English proficiency scores.

IELTS: 6+ with minimum of 5.5 in each section

TOEFEL: 99

Scholarships: Bocconi offers tuition discounts based on family income and assets of less than $156,019.50 (127,000 euros) per year. Depending on the bracket the family income falls in, the reduced tuition rate is $6,761.66 (5,504 euros); $9,538.07 (7,764 euros); or $12,351.34 (10,054 euros) per year.

In addition, Bocconi has merit-based scholarships for international students ranging from a 50% tuition waiver to a full scholarship that includes housing costs. All international candidates are considered.

Bocconi also has a FAFSA number! This is a huge advantage to American students, as it allows them to utilize US funding options for college in Italy and use their 529 savings without penalty.

English-taught bachelor's programs:

International Economics and Management	3 years	12,324 euros ($15,140.03) per year
International Economics and Finance	3 years	12,324 euros ($15,140.03) per year
Economics and Social Sciences	3 years	12,324 euros ($15,140.03) per year
Economics, Management, and Computer Science	3 years	12,324 euros ($15,140.03) per year
Economics and Management for Arts, Culture, and Communication	3 years	12,324 euros ($15,140.03) per year
World Bachelor in Business	4 years	24,595* euros ($30,214.96) per year
International Politics and Government	3 years	12,324 euros ($15,140.03) per year

* The tuition for this program changes according to the location each year. Price listed is the average if choice year is spent at Bocconi.

Interested in Learning More about College in Europe?

As a book purchaser, you have access to the College Beyond the States companion website. Visit www.collegebeyondthestates.com and enter access code Global2018. You will find photos and contact information for each of the schools listed.

Of course, there are many excellent options beyond the schools listed in this book. Beyond the States members have access to our searchable database of all the 1700+ accredited, English-taught bachelor's degree programs in continental Europe. Members benefit from monthly Q&A calls with Jennifer Viemont and have options that include consultations and personalized lists of best fit programs or study areas. You can learn more about membership options at www.beyondthestates.com

Email media@beyondthestates.com if you are interested in having Jennifer as a speaker at your event, on your podcast, radio or television program.

Suggested Reading

Colleges That Change Lives: 40 Schools That Will Change the Way You Look At Colleges, by Loren Pope. 4th ed (Penguin Books, 2012)

This groundbreaking book was first published in 2000 and is now in its 4th edition. The book provides information about lesser-known schools that address some of the issues of American higher education, including the high selectivity and quality issues. While this book does an excellent job at exposing and promoting unfamiliar yet high quality options, affordability is not addressed as the average tuition for the profiled schools is more than $30k per year.

Where You Go Is Not Who You'll Be: An Antidote to the College Admissions Mania, by Frank Bruni (Grand Central Publishing, 2016)

This compelling book discusses the problems around putting too much emphasis on brand name schools. The author shows research and case studies that counter this mindset and speaks to the many flaws in the US higher education admissions process. Like Pope's book, this book does a wonderful job encouraging families to look beyond big-name schools and considering factors other than prestige when selecting a school.

Beyond Measure: Rescuing an Overscheduled, Overtested, Underestimated Generation, by Vicki Abeles (Simon &Schuster, 2016)

Following up from her trailblazing documentary, *Race to Nowhere,* Abeles maintains that the primary and secondary educational systems are harming students. She profiles families, communities, and schools that are making changes to benefit students. Unfortunately, families that make some of these changes will limit their choices as it pertains to higher education in the US. The transparent and objective European admissions system allows for American students to maintain balance in their life.

Excellent Sheep: The Miseducation of the American Elite and the Way to a Meaningful Life, by William Deresiewicz (Free Press, 2015)

The author, a professor at Yale, argues that the college admissions process as well as the education students get in elite colleges are creating conformists who lack critical, independent, and creative thinking skills. His premise is that true liberal arts programs provide the solution needed. Despite the reduced emphasis on the humanities, many European programs have the qualities that Deresiewicz calls out as strengths of the ideal liberal arts education.

Most Likely to Succeed: Preparing Our Kids for the Innovation Era, by Tony Wagner and Ted Dintersmith (Scribner, 2016).

The authors call for a reform of our outdated educational system, providing evidence that even students who graduate with high credentials are not prepared for success in the twenty-first-century economy.

Crazy U: One Dad's Crash Course in Getting His Kid into College, by Andrew Ferguson (Simon & Schuster, 2012)

This very readable memoir follows a father's investigation into the various hoops his son encounters through the college admissions process. It exposes and explains the problems related to the admissions process, including flaws around the *US News* rankings, SATs, application essays, financial aid, and college costs. The relatable writing style makes is easy to understand the problems around US higher education.

Academically Adrift: Limited Learning on College Campuses by Richard Arun and Josipa Roksa 2011, University of Chicago Press

The authors of this book conducted extensive research to explore the learning gains made by students at American universities. Packed with troubling findings, this book found that 36% of the students did not show gains in a number of skills, including critical thinking, complex reasoning, and writing over their four years at college, proving that many American college students are simply not getting their money's worth.

Fail U: The False Promise of Higher Education, by Charles Sykes (St. Martin's Press, 2016)

If you can read only one book off this list, it should be this one. The book provides a thorough summary and research around many of the major problems of higher education, particularly around the educational problems and deficiencies on American campuses. Sykes looks at such things as skyrocketing tuition, burned out or inept professors, and the fact that more students than ever are graduating college lacking the fundamental skills they need to succeed.

Endnotes

1   Sykes, Charles. *Fail U.: The Promise of Higher Education.* New York: St. Martin's Press, 2016.

2   Coley, Richard, Madeline J. Goodman and Anita M. Sands. "America's Skills Challenge: Millenials and the Future." ETS. Accessed April 19, 2018. https://www.ets.org/s/research/29836/.

3   Selingo, Jeffrey J. "Is college worth the cost? Many recent graduates don't think so." The Washington Post. Accessed April 7, 2018. https://www.washingtonpost.com/news/grade-point/wp/2015/09/30/is-college-worth-the-cost-many-recent-graduates-dont-think-so/?utm_term=.4c07156034b8.

4   Arun, Richard and Josipa Roska. *Academically Adrift: Limited Learning on College Campuses.* Chicago: University of Chicago Press, 2011.

5   Riley, Naomi Schaefer. *The Faculty Lounges: And Other Reasons You Won't Get the College Education You Pay For.* Place of Publication Not Identified: Rowman & Littlefield, 2015.

6   Sellingo, Jeffrey. (2016) There is Life After College: What Parents and Students Should Know About Navigating School to Prepare for the Jobs of Tomorrow, William Morrow Publishing.

7   Kolet, Michelle Jamrisko and Ilan. "Cost of College Degree in US Soars 12 Fold: Chart of the Day." Bloomberg.com. August 15, 2012. Accessed April 19, 2018. https://www.bloomberg.com/news/articles/2012-08-15/cost-of-college-degree-in-u-s-soars-12-fold-chart-of-the-day.

8   Lewin, Tamar. "Most College Students Don't Earn a Degree in 4 Years, Study Finds." NyTimes.com. December 1, 2014. Accessed

April 19, 2018. https://www.nytimes.com/2014/12/02/education/most-college-students-dont-earn-degree-in-4-years-study-finds.html.

9   Korn, Melissa. "Some Elite Colleges Review an Application in 8 Minutes (or Less)". WSJ.com. January 31, 2018. Accessed April 19, 2018. https://www.wsj.com/articles/some-elite-colleges-review-an-application-in-8-minutes-or-less-1517400001.

10   Denizet-Lewis, Benoit. "Why Are More American Teenager Than Ever Suffering From Severe Anxiety?" NyTimes.com. October 11, 2017. Accessed April 7, 2018. https://www.nytimes.com/2017/10/11/magazine/why-are-more-american-teenagers-than-ever-suffering-from-severe-anxiety.html.

11   Sellingo, Jeffrey. (2016) There is Life After College: What Parents and Students Should Know About Navigating School to Prepare for the Jobs of Tomorrow, William Morrow Publishing

12   Gardner, Philip D., Georgia T. Chao, and Jessica Hurst. "Ready For Prime Time? How Internships and Co-ops Affect Decisions on Full-time Job Offers." Ceri.msu.edu. 2008. Accessed April 18, 2019. http://ceri.msu.edu/publications/pdf/internwhitep.pdf.

13   Maddux, William W., Adam D. Galinsky and Carmit T. Tadmor. "Be a Better Manager: Live Abroad." hrb.org. September 2010. Accessed April 18, 2018. https://hbr.org/2010/09/be-a-better-manager-live-abroad.

14   Farrugia, Christine. "Gaining an Employment Edge – The Impact of Study Abroad." IIE: The Power of International Education. October 2017. Accessed April 19, 2018. https://www.iie.org/en/Research-and-Insights/Publications/Gaining-an-employment-edge---The-Impact-of-Study-Abroad.

15   PISA Study: The Estonian Basic Education Is the Best in Europe." Estonian World. December 6, 2016. Accessed April 19, 2018. http://estonianworld.com/knowledge/oecd-estonian-elementary-education-best-europe/

Acknowledgements

First and foremost, I would like to thank the EU and EEA for offering international students such an abundance of high-quality and affordable higher education options!

That said, I'm so grateful for all the people who helped me with this project:

The administrators at the schools I visited who have been patient with my endless questions.

The students in Europe who have shared their enthusiasm and experiences with me.

My editor, Erica Smith, as this book would not have been possible without her invaluable and tireless assistance.

Beyond the States Members—You guys are trailblazers who are already doing this and helped me realize I needed to write this book and get the word out.

Tom, Sam, and Ellie for sharing in my excitement about this project and picking up the slack at home while I focused on this.

About the Author

Jennifer is a native of Chicago, who obtained her Master's in Social Work from the University of Illinois, Chicago. She is a Licensed Clinical Social Worker (LCSW) and has worked in a variety of areas including school social work, mental health, and coaching. Jennifer has also worked as a parenting coordinator, which is an alternative dispute resolution for high-conflict divorce cases. In addition, she has developed and implemented a program working with both high school and college students around time management, study strategies, goal setting, and other executive functioning skills that are needed for academic success. Jennifer has a passion for traveling and made it her priority to expose her kids to other countries and cultures. She loves to get a deeper feel for the cities she visits by eating, shopping, and residing in areas populated by locals. She lives in Chapel Hill, NC with her husband, two teenagers, and their two dogs.

Jennifer is the founder of Beyond the States, a resource dedicated to providing students and families a single source of information about the 1700+ English-taught bachelor's degree programs in continental Europe. Jennifer is a known expert on this topic and visits schools throughout Europe regularly, in order to provide first-hand guidance on one of the most important decisions families make. Beyond the States does not partner with any universities covered in the book or on the website, with the goal of providing objective information.

44225037R00137

Made in the USA
Middletown, DE
04 May 2019